GUO WEI

THE POWER OF TIME

TIME-MANAGEMENT PRACTICE AND REFLECTION FOR ENTERPRISES

Published by
LID Publishing
An imprint of LID Business Media Ltd.
LABS House, 15–19 Bloomsbury Way,
London, WC1A 2TH, UK

info@lidpublishing.com
www.lidpublishing.com

A member of:

businesspublishersroundtable.com

All rights reserved. Without limiting the rights under copyright reserved, no part of this publication may be reproduced, stored or introduced into a retrieval system, or transmitted, in any form or by any means (electronic, mechanical, photocopying, recording or otherwise) without the prior written permission of both the copyright owners and the publisher of this book.

This English edition is published by arrangement with LID Business Media Ltd. through the agency of China National Publications Import & Export (Group) Co., Ltd.
Project Manager: Ruilin Liu

English translation: Haiwang Yuan

© Guo Wei, 2025
© LID Business Media Limited, 2025

Printed by Gutenberg Press, Malta
ISBN: 978-1-917391-21-4
ISBN: 978-1-917391-22-1 (ebook)

Cover and page design: Caroline Li

GUO WEI

THE POWER OF TIME

**TIME-MANAGEMENT
PRACTICE AND REFLECTION
FOR ENTERPRISES**

MADRID | MEXICO CITY | LONDON
BUENOS AIRES | BOGOTA | SHANGHAI

CONTENTS

Foreword
Preface   1

CHAPTER 1
IF YOU CAN'T MANAGE TIME, YOU CAN'T MANAGE ANYTHING   6
Time Is the Scarcest Resource   7
Quality of Life Depends on Time Management   9
Time Management Is a Compulsory Course for Enterprises   13

CHAPTER 2
REEXAMINING TIME MANAGEMENT FROM A MANAGEMENT PERSPECTIVE   20
Time Management Focuses on 'Management'   21
Planning Is the Breakdown of Tasks over Time   23
Organization Is the System of Division of Tasks, Responsibilities and Processes   30
Coordination Makes Conflicts Disappear Unnoticed   34
Achieving Control Relies on Identifying Key Variables   42

CHAPTER 3
THE RIGHT APPROACH TO TIME MANAGEMENT DOUBLES EFFECTIVENESS   48
Make Good Use of Effective Time Management Tools   49
Learn How to 'List Everything'   52
Identify the Most Important 20%   58
Prioritize Tasks with Quadrants   63
Coordinate Time with a Schedule   68
Make Effective Use of Weekly Work Reports   73
Delegation Means Managing Less but Better   78
Review Effectively to Ensure Continuous Improvement   86

CHAPTER 4
SPEND TIME ON THE MOST IMPORTANT STRATEGIC MANAGEMENT — 96

Strategy Is the Core Driving Force of the Enterprise — 97
Think about Strategic Planning from a Longer Time Dimension — 99
Distinguish Priorities and Make Wise Choices — 109
Break Down Key Measures into Weekly Reports to Ensure Strategic Implementation — 113
Maintain a Proper Rhythm for Strategic Execution Without Deviation — 119
Promote the Spirit of Perseverance to Build Strategic Momentum — 123
Step Back to See the Bigger Picture and Regularly Review and Adjust — 127

CHAPTER 5
IMPROVE PROJECT MANAGEMENT EFFICIENCY THROUGH TIME MANAGEMENT — 130

Time Management Is the Soul of Project Management — 131
Plan Time Well to Ensure Project Progress — 139
Manage Stakeholders and Their Expectations: Slow Means Fast — 146
Make Good Use of Visualization Tools in Project Time Management — 150

CHAPTER 6
BUILD ORGANIZATIONAL LEADERSHIP THROUGH TIME MANAGEMENT — 158

Manage Time to Enhance Organizational Leadership — 159
Build Momentum and Believe in 'The Power of Believing' — 164
Achieve Consensus through Effective Communication — 184
Leverage the Driving Force of Incentive Mechanisms — 206
Discipline Is Combat Effectiveness — 222

CHAPTER 7
EFFECTIVENESS AND BALANCE ARE THE ULTIMATE MEANING OF TIME MANAGEMENT — 234

Focus on High Efficiency but Emphasize High Effectiveness — 235
Balance Work and Life — 238
Plan Before Taking Action to Mitigate Risks — 243

References — 247
Endnotes — 249
About the Author — 253

FOREWORD

It was M. Scott Peck who urged us to recognize the pricelessness of our only true resource. "Until you value yourself, you will not value your time," the late psychiatrist and former US Army lieutenant colonel said. "Until you value your time, you will not do anything with it."

Currency of any other type is simply a way of monetizing this most precious of finite assets. Before markets existed, centuries earlier than coins and notes, humans had sought ways to trade their time. "These potatoes cost me ten hours of my life; I shall swap them for something that cost ten hours of yours."

Lawyers, management consultants and business speakers are sometimes mocked for pricing their time precisely. The implication is that clock-watching somehow demonstrates inflexibility or an ungenerous spirit. Yet nobody reaches their final hours wishing they had wasted more of those that went before. Money is a liquid asset – should we run short of it, we can find ways to earn more. Nobody – prince or pauper – can create more time. It waits for no one.

At *Dialogue* magazine, we explore ways to make business better, smarter, more successful. The theories and ideas we promote are cyphers for every organization making the most of the days it is given; ensuring that its people are engaged and enlivened, producing their best work in a timescale that both keeps the business ahead of its competition and allows those people space for rest and leisure. Time is shared: optimization, not maximization, is the secret to success.

Few in business would refute these truths. Yet still too much time is wasted. The hours squandered by the world's businesses are shocking. According to *Forbes*, the average employee spends 31 hours a week in unproductive meetings. Most of the week is worked without gain.

Guo Wei, founder of Digital China, knows it is time to save time. *The Power of Time* presents Digital China's enterprise management theoretical framework based on time management. The book provides a classic methodology that extends from personal time management to leveraging time management as a tool for corporate strategic management.

Guo outlines Seven Essentials of Time Management, but more importantly, he combines these principles with successful management practices. He systematically explains a methodological framework for enhancing corporate strategic management capabilities and organizational leadership. The book introduces an original organizational leadership model, based on Potential x Transmission x Mechanism x Discipline. This model guides enterprises in continuously strengthening organizational alignment and improving organizational efficiency.

In the opening passage of the book, Guo writes that "Resources are limited, while human desires and needs are infinite." It is a fact too easily forgotten. The role of business leaders is to find ways to meet demand with a finite supply of this most precious resource. *The Power of Time* is a great place to start.

Patrick Woodman is editor of *Dialogue*

Dialogue magazine offers a broad range of insight, analysis and ideas on the challenges facing leaders today, on themes spanning leadership and people management, strategy, innovation and technology, marketing and sales, and finance. It is the house journal of Duke University's Duke Corporate Education.

PREFACE

Digital China[1] was born in a unique historical context. From the very first day, it faced enormous challenges, necessitating a fight for survival. At that time, Digital China was like a small boat, navigating through the tumultuous waves of the external environment while continuously evolving and upgrading during its transformation. Sometimes, I even thought that starting a new entrepreneurial venture from scratch might be easier than leading the transformation of traditional business operations, as the inertia of history can easily stifle the vitality of innovation.

Starting a business is arduous, but we have persevered for 24 fleeting years. I feel gratified to see that Digital China has evolved from a small boat into a large ship. This ship now carries not only 20,000 employees but also our partners and customers, making us both a community of shared interests and a community of shared destiny. We strive to steer this ship steadily and farther so that everyone on board can lead a happier life, achieve greater personal value, and continuously pursue honor and dreams – bringing the vision of a 'Digital China' to reality.

During this transformation, I have maintained a consistent expectation for Digital China: From the margins to the mainstream and from the mainstream to the forefront. What do the margins and the mainstream refer to? In the early days, we were engaged in IT product agency distribution, which, although related to technology, was a marginal business. Of course, in the early 21st century, when the market's understanding of IT was quite limited, this was a good cash-flow business. It was precisely because of this business that Digital China survived. However, we never forgot that transitioning to IT services, developing software services and providing digital solutions to our customers was the core of the IT business. For this, we worked hard for over two decades, not only successfully entering the mainstream but also achieving leadership positions in related fields. Today, Data Cloud Integration is the future direction of digital technology development. Digital China has embarked on a new journey, advancing to the forefront of technology and working hard to provide customers with autonomous and globally synchronized data-cloud-integrated infrastructure technology, products and services.

This presents a challenge to our organizational capabilities: How can we ensure that our team more efficiently engages in exploring cutting-edge technologies? How can we empower each employee to realize their maximum potential? How can we effectively manage strategy to ensure it is truly implemented and generates strategic momentum? How can we optimally allocate the limited internal resources of the enterprise to achieve organizational goals better? How can we establish organizational leadership?

To find answers to these questions, I extensively studied classic management books written by management gurus. We are fortunate to live in an era rich in knowledge resources, with many management theories worthy of our study and reference. From Fredrick Winslow Taylor and Taylorism to Elton Mayo's law, from Chester Barnard to Herbert Simon, management theories and methods have continuously evolved based on different assumptions about people. Learning these theories has provided me with much inspiration, and Peter F. Drucker's *The Effective Executive* had a particularly profound impact on me. However, how can so many theories and methods be applied to the enterprise? What is the key to management in enterprises? As a practitioner, I have always been trying to find a simple yet efficient key to enterprise management.

One day, while reading Tagore's book discussing the meaning of life, I suddenly realized that everyone is in pursuit of the meaning of life. And what is life? Isn't it just time? Whether viewed from an individual or organizational perspective, time is a nonrenewable resource. If we can make every day meaningful, doesn't that make life more meaningful? At that moment, I had an epiphany: Time management was the effective key to enterprise management that I had been searching for!

Following this line of thought, I began to organize and summarize various time management theories and methods. I initiated training programs at different levels within the company, encouraging everyone to learn and discuss these concepts. I also promoted time management tools, such as weekly reports, throughout the company. Through a variety of methods, we collectively learned about time management and considered how to improve our work efficiency. Over time, scientific and efficient time management gradually became part of our corporate culture. From 2017 to now, we have continuously practised, summarized and engaged in collective thinking and validation. Ultimately, we developed a systematic and practical time management methodology, which led to the creation of this book.

The first edition of this book was written in 2017 and used as training material within the company. In 2021, the second edition was compiled, updating the original content and incorporating many excellent case studies about time management from within the company. During this process, many colleagues provided me with assistance, for which I am grateful. Therefore, this book is a product of practical enterprise management, as well as a result of team spirit and collective effort. It embodies the hard work of countless people and serves as a management guide jointly written by the people of Digital China.

Since its inception with a few billion RMB (renminbi, also known as the Chinese Yuan) to today's 150 billion RMB, Digital China has navigated through numerous challenges, advancing from the margins to the forefront. In this great, once-in-a-century trend, we have taken time management as our key tool. With confidence and determination, we aim to achieve unique value for Digital China at critical points in the global digital industry chain and contribute our due share to the digital transformation of China.

The opportunities in life depend on whom you are with. I am fortunate to have been blessed with kind parents who not only gave me life but also taught me the principles of being a good person. I am lucky to have received guidance from numerous top professors and scholars during my studies; they are masters in their respective fields and have instilled in me the habit of drawing strength from classics and the courage to pursue knowledge. I am fortunate to have received mentorship from a leader-level entrepreneur of the first generation in China's era of reform, which opened up when I joined my first company. I am grateful to the company's board of directors for continuously encouraging me to move forward and challenging my intellect during the company's trial-and-error process ... I am, therefore, filled with gratitude.

I want to thank the team members who have worked hard alongside me. Every time we overcame difficulties together, it brought me a sense of elevation, and every time we celebrated together, it was the best experience of my life. I also want to thank my family. It is hard for someone focused on work to balance life and work, but without the joy of life, there would be no passion for work. It is their tolerance and selfless support that allowed me to fully commit to the practice of enterprise management and achieve success and reflection. The Chinese edition of this book was published in 2023 by the Enterprise Management Publishing House. After its release, the time management practices presented in the book received the 2023 Ram Charan Management Practice Award, the highest award for management practices in China. Now, the English edition is also published. We would like to extend our gratitude to the translator Haiwang Yuan, CNPIEC (China National Publications Import and Export (Groups) Co., Ltd.), and LID Business Media for their strong support, which has been instrumental in the successful publication of this book.

Previously, after the release of my other book, *The Power of Datafication*, my friend Zhang Gaobo, cofounder of Micro Connect, wrote to me: "While reading Chapter 3, 'Digital Transformation Driven By Data Cloud Integration,' the real-life scenarios of Micro Connect kept surfacing in my mind. It felt like you were writing about Micro Connect! Data asset accumulation, inter-industry data sharing, AI-powered decision-making, and boundaryless organization are exactly the directions of our work. Your articulation has made everything so clear!"

I sincerely hope that *The Power of Time* will resonate with readers just as profoundly. At the same time, I kindly invite readers to offer criticism and corrections for any omissions or inaccuracies found within the book.

Guo Wei
June 2024

CHAPTER 1

IF YOU CAN'T MANAGE TIME, YOU CAN'T MANAGE ANYTHING

TIME IS THE SCARCEST RESOURCE

Economics has a core concept called 'scarcity.' What is scarcity? Economist Thomas Sowell has given a brilliant explanation: "There has never been enough to satisfy everyone completely. That is the real constraint. That is what scarcity means."[2] Resources are limited, while human desires and needs are infinite. The conflict and contradiction between these two are the fundamental issues that economics seeks to address. Among all natural and social resources, there is one that is the scarcest, and that is time.

The scarcity of time lies in its absolute fairness. No one can gain even an extra second; time is the most equitable resource bestowed upon us by heaven. However, in the long run, everyone's lifespan varies, resulting in different total amounts of time. In the short term, whether rich or poor, old or young, everyone has only 24 hours a day. No one can have more, not even by 0.1 seconds; whether you work tirelessly or are lazy and slack, your allotted time neither increases nor decreases.

The scarcity of time lies in its irreversibility. In classical physics, Newton proposed the concept of absolute space and time. In his work *Mathematical Principles of Natural Philosophy*, he described time as: "Absolute, true and mathematical time, of itself, and from its nature, flows equably without regard to anything external." According to Newton, "Time is like a river that flows uniformly without beginning or end." It is absolute, infinite, always moving forward, never pausing and never stopping. Over 2,000 years before Newton, the Eastern philosopher Confucius expressed the same sentiment: "Time passes like a river, flowing unceasingly day and night." Due to this irreversibility, once time is gone, it will never return.

The scarcity of time lies in its complete inflexibility. There are only so many hours in a day; we cannot 'increase supply' nor 'cut demand.' We can only use these 24 hours to create value. No matter how many demands you have, time will not increase its supply. If you do not cherish and make good use of time, life will pass by in vain, and you will ultimately accomplish nothing.

The scarcity of time also lies in its irreplaceability. To some extent, we can use one resource to replace another, such as using new energy sources to power cars instead of petrol or using plastic steel profiles instead of wood to make furniture. However, nothing possesses the properties of time, which cannot be replaced by anything else.

More importantly, time is the soil from which everything in the world grows. Humans and all beings in nature are born, grow, age and die within the continuum of time. All the values and achievements created by humanity are products of time. Without time, life loses its meaning.

Therefore, as Peter F. Drucker said, "Time is the scarcest resource, and unless it is managed, nothing else can be managed."

QUALITY OF LIFE DEPENDS ON TIME MANAGEMENT

Time is so scarce and precious that we often say, "Time is life." How we manage time determines the quality of our lives.

Many people feel resentment and dissatisfaction due to inequalities in status, thought, wealth and other social discourse systems. In fact, time resources are equal for everyone, but due to poor management of these resources, there are significant differences in the quality of life among individuals. In real life, I often see many people wasting a considerable amount of time on trivial, meaningless things, idly passing their days in a haze. Whenever this happens, I can't help but recall what Peter F. Drucker said in *The Effective Executive*: "We are all consumers of time, and most of us also tend to be time wasters!" When these people complain and regret their mediocrity and lack of achievements, do they realize that it is all because they squander and waste their time?

In contrast, those who have made outstanding achievements in a particular field all treat time as precious and have a deep understanding of time management. Throughout history, great scientists and masters of the arts, who have created material and spiritual wealth for humanity, have regarded time as a treasure and seized every minute and second. Many entrepreneurs I know are also like this.

For those who know how to cherish time and make good use of it, life is a prolonged battle against its scarcity. The scarcer the time, the more they strive to seize every moment and make the most of their life, aiming to improve time utilization and create greater value. Especially in today's era, which increasingly values speed and efficiency, it is crucial to invest limited temporal resources in more meaningful activities. Their achievements are determined by their time management.

Time wasters and those who cherish time may make different choices because of their various understandings of 'the value of human existence.'

What is the value of human existence? Anyone who has deeply pondered this question will no longer live a chaotic and wasteful life.

In my view, the value of human existence depends on both one's social attributes and inner attributes. If we weigh the importance of these two aspects, the latter may play a greater role in determining how one realizes the value of life. In other words, inner attributes largely determine whether a person's intelligence and talents can be fully utilized, allowing them to live a life that is true to themselves and beneficial to society, or at least make some contributions to society.

So, how can one achieve the value of life by adjusting inner attributes? Tagore's perspective on this matter is worth considering. He stated that a person encompasses three interdependent aspects: life, intellect and mind.

Life is limited, so we should strive to extend its length and broaden its width. To extend a limited life, one must ensure good health. If the body is unhealthy, especially if one suffers from a serious illness, it is easy to fall into despair and lose the desire to think or act, and everything will become meaningless.

To broaden the width of life, one must enhance the quality of life. The quality of life mainly depends on whether a person possesses profound knowledge and moral integrity and can create value for society. Lu Xun, a famed early 20th-century Chinese progressive writer, once said that quality of life is more important than the length of life. This viewpoint is correct: Compared to longevity, it is more important to pursue the quality of life, to do meaningful things every day, even every moment, and to achieve progress in intellect and mind. This way, life becomes more valuable, and one's sense of happiness increases.

Intellect, or human perception or worldview, lasts longer than the duration of life itself. Humans are a fascinating species, continuously learning new knowledge after birth, eventually becoming increasingly intelligent, and undergoing significant changes in their understanding of the world. Thus, humans are a fusion of life and intellect.

For example, Stephen Richards Covey wrote *The 7 Habits of Highly Effective People*, a book that has remained popular even after his lifetime. Similarly, Henry Ford founded the Ford Motor Company, a business that has remained successful beyond his lifespan.

How can we grow our intellect? The principle is simple: It depends on the growth of the mind, which means enhancing our understanding of the value of our inner world. In fact, although the scope and extent may vary, every person's mind can influence society. For example, a team leader has a significant influence on team members – the leader's perception and feelings about the world translate into actions, create an atmosphere and affect the team members.

How does the mind grow? Through thinking. Wang Yangming, a prominent philosopher of the Ming dynasty, advocated the concept of *gewu zhizhi*, meaning to investigate the nature of things to acquire knowledge. If the mind is constantly numb and fuzzy, intellectual growth is impossible. At Digital China, we encourage hard work, but this doesn't mean mechanically repeating tasks; it means thinking thoughtfully. Many great achievements often seem to come from sudden inspiration, but they are the result of extensive contemplation.

Netflix is the world's largest streaming service provider. There is a widely circulated version of its startup story: Netflix cofounder Reed Hastings rented a movie from the Blockbuster platform but had to pay a $40 late fee because he returned it late. This sparked an idea in him: "What if there was a platform that didn't charge late fees?" Thus, Netflix was born. However, Hastings had spent a long time thinking about startup ideas before this, such as custom baseball bats and personalized surfboards, and had made many attempts to succeed with these. Turning the initial concept of Netflix into reality involved months of intense discussion and in-depth research by Hastings and his startup team. They held several marathon meetings in a family restaurant. The business legend of Netflix may seem like a coincidence, almost like the mind having a momentary handshake and conversation with God. But in fact, its creation and development were the results of Hastings's long-term contemplation and accumulation of ideas.

When understanding the relationship between life, intellect and mind, people realize that everyone's time is limited. However, within this limited time, one can achieve growth in intellect and mind by accomplishing valuable tasks. The rate of development of the latter two depends on the ability to manage time and whether there is enough time to do these things.

In our life journey, the time we have is limited, and our actions must adhere to various tangible or intangible rules, with no possibility of turning back. Our work in a particular industry, company or department is just a segment of this journey, requiring us to seek out the rules of industry development and adhere to company management regulations. However, during this journey, the freedom and growth of our intellect and mind are limitless, unrestricted by time and place. This freedom and growth depend on how well we utilize our time. If we can make every minute and second of our lives fully valuable, our lives will undoubtedly have a higher quality.

TIME MANAGEMENT IS A COMPULSORY COURSE FOR ENTERPRISES

Individual time management is of great significance. Similarly, the development of enterprises also depends on time management. Compared to personal growth, competition between enterprises is more brutal; it can be said that it's a matter of life and death. This requires enterprises to seize opportunities at all times, capturing opportunities faster and in less time than competitors to gain a foothold in the market.

However, if I were to ask, "What is the most important thing in an enterprise?" I believe many people would provide a variety of answers, such as talent, marketing, strategy, customers, capital and so on, but very few would answer "time."

Through years of observation, I have found that most enterprises and most people within them do not recognize the importance of time as a resource, nor have they established a scientific and clear concept of time despite its presence in every work environment and stage. When categorizing an enterprise's management content, few managers would list 'time management' separately, and even fewer would regard it as an important part of their management work.

It's essential to understand that time is of paramount importance for enterprises. Within the same time frame, enterprises can create significantly more wealth than individuals. Time for enterprises signifies efficiency, effectiveness and productivity. From a cost perspective, time is equally significant. While it may seem that time has no direct cost for enterprises, the reality is that the most substantial and expensive resource continuously invested in operations is the time of managers and employees. If time management in the enterprise is not executed effectively, it hampers the team's coordination, and the time invested by managers and employees becomes a sunk cost, wasted in vain.

Therefore, managing time is as important in enterprises as managing people, finances and materials. So, what value does time management bring to enterprises? Based on my experience in enterprise management, it can be summarized in three points.

1. IMPROVE THE EFFICIENCY OF TEAM COORDINATION

In enterprises, most tasks are interdependent. When the work at one process node is not completed, the next process node can only wait. If too much time is spent waiting, the overall efficiency of the team will be greatly affected.

Using an Activity on Edge (AOE) Network (see Figure 1-1), we can clearly and intuitively see the overall time consumption of team collaboration.

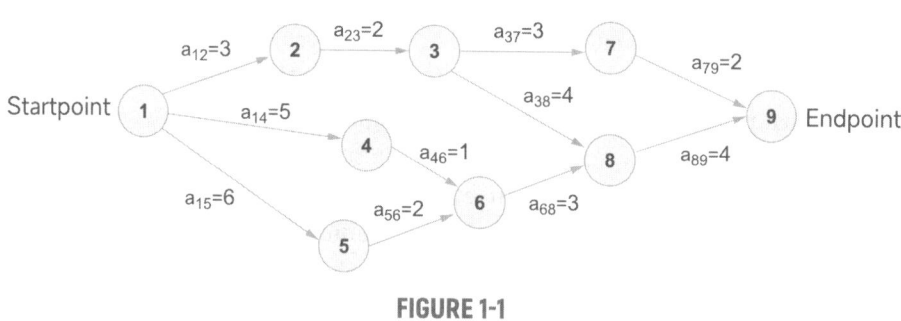

FIGURE 1-1
AOE NETWORK EXAMPLE

An AOE Network[3] is used to estimate the overall time required for a combination of activities. The diagram contains two types of symbols: circles and arrows. The circles represent nodes, and the arrows (also called edges) represent processes. The numbers marked on the edges represent the time required for the process. If we consider Node One as the starting point and Node Nine as the endpoint, each node's occurrence has its prerequisites, and subsequent nodes can only be reached after the preceding activities have occurred. For example, Node Six can only happen after both a_{46} and a_{56} have been completed. By following the event flow in the diagram, we can identify the critical path to complete the task and determine the time required from Node One to Node Nine.

This is a mathematical tool for performing quantitative analysis of project schedules, commonly used in detailed project management. Here, we will not consider quantitative analysis but will look at it qualitatively. If there are bottlenecks or delays in the activities on the critical path, the progress of the entire process will be delayed. This visual representation helps us better understand the importance of time management in team collaboration.

Within an enterprise, the coordination between various departments and activities consistently applies the concept of collaboration and involves aspects of time management. To fully seize business opportunities, internal business and functional departments need to collaborate effectively. Every member must realize that personal time is not just individual time but also team time. A single oversight or mistake by an individual can lead to significant time wastage for the entire team. Everyone should strive to avoid becoming a bottleneck in team collaboration.

If the entire team's time can be managed through scientific time management, creating resonance and synergy among members, the team's coordination efficiency and the enterprise's time utilization efficiency will be greatly improved, thereby generating an effect of '1 + 1 > 2.'

2. SAVE CUSTOMERS' TIME AND IMPROVE CUSTOMER SERVICE EFFICIENCY

For enterprises, time management has another important significance: It can save customers time and improve customer service efficiency. The importance of customers is self-evident. As Peter Drucker said, "The customer is the foundation of a business and keeps it in existence. The customer alone gives employment. Society entrusts resources that create wealth to businesses in order to meet customer needs." In this sense, saving customers' time is also an important way to provide service to them.

ITL New Logistics, a smart supply chain service brand under Digital China Holdings,[4] started by providing supply chain services for IT products to major manufacturers and expanded to offer smart warehousing services for the consumer goods industry. It quickly secured many leading clients in various sectors precisely because it adhered to the concept of 'saving time for customers' and achieved effective time management.

When providing smart warehousing services to customers, ITL New Logistics tracks the time from order receipt to goods dispatch. By continuously compressing this time, they improve service efficiency for customers, on the one hand, and enhance labor utilization within the warehouse to reduce costs on the other. Here, I will use a typical client of ITL New Logistics, Company P, as an example to illustrate the challenges of such services.

Company P is a world-leading consumer goods company with many trusted leading brands. Company Y in Beijing, the largest global distributor for Company P, is responsible for its e-commerce business on a certain online platform. Every year during 'Double 11,'[5] the massive volume of orders presents a huge challenge for Company Y's supply chain management, necessitating the need for a third-party professional logistics company to improve service quality and customer satisfaction. In the online sales of fast-moving consumer goods, 'speed' is the

most important service element emphasized by the brand. For the operation of Company P's Tmall store, fast delivery involves numerous practical difficulties:
1. Rapid and significant changes in product categories and activity demand quantities;
2. Complex Stock Keeping Unit (SKU) assortment and a wide variety of promotional gifts require high accuracy in warehouse operations;
3. Frequent promotions with large peak order volumes demand high efficiency in warehouse operations;
4. Wide delivery areas necessitate a high on-time delivery rate;
5. Fragile items in the cleaning and care product category require high packaging quality.

Since 2014, ITL New Logistics has maintained a close partnership with Company Y. To provide faster and better services, ITL New Logistics has comprehensively improved its warehouse network layout, precise forecasting and operational capabilities, continuously enhancing outbound efficiency.

In terms of warehouse network layout, ITL New Logistics has rapidly expanded from a single warehouse in North China to nine warehouses nationwide, covering the entire country. During peak periods, they can quickly scale up to 21 warehouses for dispatch, efficiently responding to customer needs locally and minimizing delivery times. Regarding precise forecasting, they swiftly adapt to marketing strategies, accurately analyse and establish pre-packaging mechanisms, and prepare packaging work ahead of peak order arrivals, achieving a pre-packaged sell-through rate of 89%. In terms of operational capabilities, they continuously upgrade management systems, including warehouse management systems, work order management systems and big data service platforms, enhancing in-warehouse work efficiency and consistently providing faster services to customers.

As a result of the collaboration between ITL New Logistics, Company P and Company Y over the years, from 2016 to 2021, the peak order growth rate during the period of Tmall's Single's Day or Double 11 marketing campaign reached 409%.

The number of Company P's brands used in operation has expanded from just one to over five. From 2019 to 2021, the full-link delivery time during the Double 11 period was reduced by 28%, with delivery times improving from five days to less than two days for all shipments.

Brand owners aim to provide consumers with a faster e-commerce delivery experience, and Company Y strives to offer quicker e-commerce delivery operations. This demand is transmitted to ITL New Logistics, which must implement a series of measures to bring faster delivery to customers and, ultimately, to end consumers. In this supply chain, 'saving time' is the most important reason customers continue to choose ITL New Logistics, and it is the gold standard upon which ITL New Logistics' smart supply chain services are based.

3. ACHIEVING SYNCHRONIZATION AND INTEGRATION OF ENTERPRISE DEVELOPMENT AND EMPLOYEE PERSONAL DEVELOPMENT

Enterprises have their development plans, and employees have their career development plans. When these two align, employees and the company can grow together, achieve mutual success and realize a win-win situation. In this process, time management plays a significant role. For example, Digital China has developed detailed strategic plans for company development, including both long-term and short-term plans. Each stage of the company's development has clear goals and a road map for achieving those goals. If employees can align their career development plans with the company's strategic objectives based on their circumstances, they can achieve synchronization and integration of enterprise development and personal growth, unleashing greater value for the entire organization.

In a sense, competition between enterprises is also a competition of time. If a company cannot manage its time well, using only 30% of its time to compete against another company's 100% time, how can it possibly win? The companies that can stand firm in market competition and even become leaders are certainly those that have perfected time management. This is precisely why I place great importance on time management and even consider it a part of the company culture.

CHAPTER 2
REEXAMINING TIME MANAGEMENT FROM A MANAGEMENT PERSPECTIVE

TIME MANAGEMENT FOCUSES ON 'MANAGEMENT'

Since time management is so important, what exactly is time management? When discussing time management, many people focus on 'time,' but from my perspective, the emphasis of time management should be on 'management.'

What is management? Management can be an action or a process. It is both a practice and a science. It involves resource allocation and the execution of the will. It includes a range of methods and covers numerous subjects. Theoretically, management is a complex matter.

It may not align perfectly with etymological theory, but I prefer to interpret the essence of management through the English word 'manage' in a far-fetched manner. The combination of 'man' and 'age' suggests that management is about human maturity. Maturity, in this sense, is the ability to understand oneself and the surrounding environment, reflecting the philosophical demands that management places on individuals. To measure a person's management level and competence, one should consider their maturity. A manager's maturity is evident in various dimensions such as the market, technology, marketing, brand operations and human resource management, and it usually correlates with their management abilities. Simply put, a higher level of maturity in a manager signifies stronger management capabilities. Conversely, a lower level of maturity indicates insufficient management skills.

The purpose of management is to enhance the maturity of individuals and organizations. To achieve this goal, managers need to coordinate others' activities through four main functions: planning, organizing, coordinating and controlling.[6] These functions form the four major functions of management (see Figure 2-1).

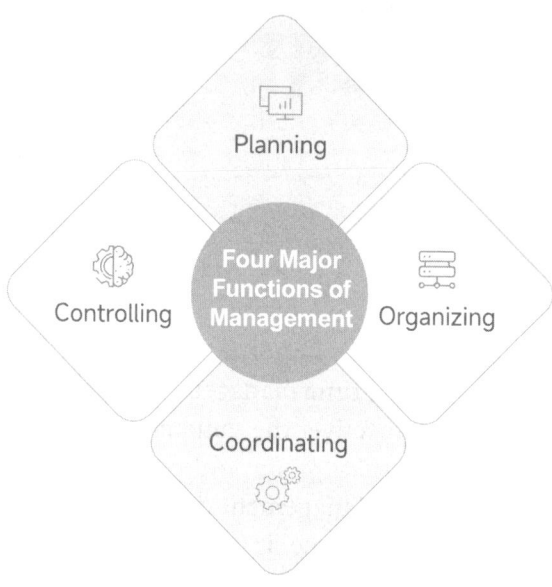

FIGURE 2-1
THE FOUR MAJOR FUNCTIONS OF MANAGEMENT

From a managerial perspective, time management takes on a new understanding: It involves managing time through actions such as planning, organizing, coordinating and controlling. This approach mobilizes the enthusiasm and efficiency of each team member, fosters effective collaboration and enhances the team's execution capabilities, thereby enabling the organization to achieve its expected goals more quickly and effectively.

In business practice, management is a cyclical and ongoing process. The four basic functions – planning, organizing, coordinating and controlling – are closely interconnected. Next, we will discuss each of these functions in detail.

PLANNING IS THE BREAKDOWN OF TASKS OVER TIME

Planning is a fundamental function of management and initiates the entire management process. With a plan in place, other management functions carried out by managers have a solid foundation, guiding various activities within the organization.

In time management, planning is equally important. For any company aiming to achieve higher efficiency, planning is essential. It involves allocating time to different tasks or, conversely, assigning tasks to different time slots (similar to IP allocation in computer networks). This allows everyone in the organization to clearly understand who needs to do what, when and where to do it, and how to achieve the goals. Managers can better understand the measures subordinates need to take to complete their work objectives, identify any issues and determine the necessary support and guidance. This enables managers to monitor and control the progress and completion of tasks, ensuring that work proceeds in an orderly manner, goals are ultimately achieved, and chaos and disorder are avoided.

Of course, the prerequisite for allocation is listing the tasks. As Peter Drucker said, "Effective executives do not start with their tasks. They start with their time. And they do not start with planning. They start by finding out where their time actually goes." By listing tasks and clearly understanding what needs to be done, time allocation becomes more reasonable and effective.

After listing the tasks, they need to be categorized based on their importance and urgency. Then, according to their importance and urgency, tasks should be scheduled into different time slots. The challenge in planning lies in the limited availability of time and the conflicts between multiple tasks. We need to anticipate these conflicts as much as possible and plan and coordinate accordingly. Such arrangements are often not perfect, and making trade-offs becomes a frequent issue we must face.

How to make plans for better utilization of time is a concern for many managers. Some people make plans by directly filling tasks into a calendar, but we do not recommend this approach. Why? Because when making plans, time is not the core; the task is the core, and the premise of the task is the goal. Simply planning according to a calendar often leads to forgetting important things. If we start by analysing goals in detail, breaking each goal down into tasks, and then considering other factors such as funding, stakeholders, resources and time expenditure, we can place tasks into appropriate time slots more reliably. Therefore, our weekly report system (see Figure 2-2) is designed to list goals first, then break them down into tasks, and finally fill them into the timetable.

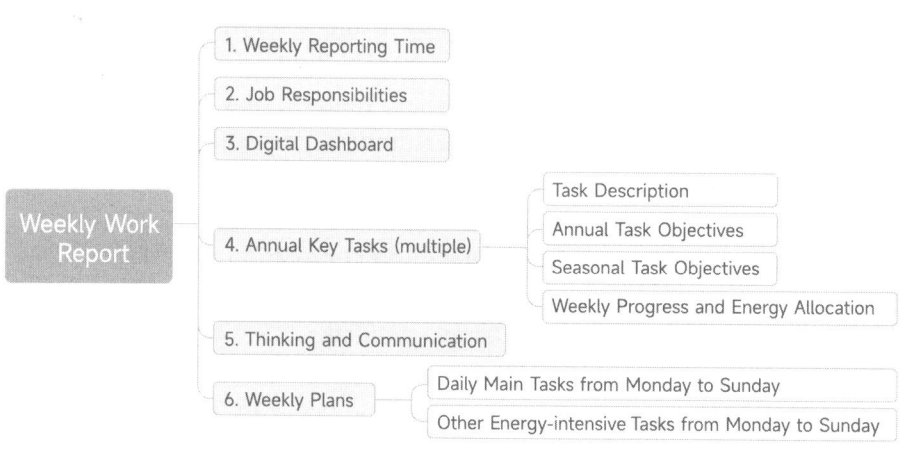

FIGURE 2-2
STRUCTURE OF THE WEEKLY REPORT SYSTEM
(2022 EDITION) BY DIGITAL CHINA

Specifically, a plan should include four key points:

1. WHAT TO DO

Before making a plan, it is essential to define the work goals clearly. Then, list the tasks that need to be completed within the specified time frame to achieve these goals, along with the specific requirements. The more detailed and clear the description, the better.

2. HOW TO DO IT

To complete the tasks and achieve the goals, what measures and strategies should be taken? These should be clearly outlined in the plan, as they guarantee its implementation. Measures and strategies mainly refer to the methods needed to reach the set goals, including mobilizing forces, obtaining resources, seeking help from others, creating suitable conditions and overcoming difficulties. Managers should comprehensively arrange these measures based on objective conditions, detailing the 'how to do it' in the plan and ensuring they are practical. Solutions should be pre-planned for potential problems that may arise during the goal achievement process.

3. WHO WILL DO IT

It is crucial to clarify who is responsible for each step of the plan and assign tasks properly to ensure that each task has a specific person committed to implementing it and taking responsibility. This way, tasks can be effectively carried out. If the plan cannot be completed or problems arise, the responsible person can be identified to accelerate corrections.

Most tasks consist of multiple steps, which are often interwoven. Therefore, when making the plan, it is necessary to consider the overall picture, carefully deciding which tasks should be done first and which should be done later, which tasks should be assigned to the most capable team members, and which tasks can be delayed slightly.

4. WHEN TO DO IT

Each step of the plan should specify deadlines so that all relevant departments and personnel clearly understand when they should complete their tasks and what the negative impacts of delays would be.

Next, let's take the delivery plan management of the CORE Banking system of the Digital China Information Service Group Co. Ltd. (DCITS)[7] as an example of how a scientific and effective plan can be formulated.

The delivery of a CORE Banking system project can take a year or even longer, involving a team of over a hundred people working together. The project manager is responsible not only for managing their own tasks and time but also for coordinating the tasks and schedules of project team members, third-party companies and hundreds of people involved in banking operations and technology. The quality of the plan greatly impacts the execution and outcome of the project.

From the perspective of the Waterfall Model, the custom development and delivery of a CORE Banking system project can be divided into four major phases: requirements analysis, design and development, integration testing and trial operation. This project involves thousands of tasks that need to be listed using a Gantt chart.[8] It's essential to identify the critical paths of these tasks, align them with the schedule, assign them to individuals and establish a project organizational structure. This organization enables everyone to work in an orderly manner, with planning playing a crucial role. How do project managers create effective plans, particularly in listing tasks and identifying key points?

First, the key to planning is task decomposition. While there are methodologies and tools such as brainstorming, expert judgement and mind mapping, determining the granularity of tasks and the principles of decomposition can be challenging and are often not well-mastered.

Typically, tasks should be decomposed to the point where they are independent, can be executed by a single person, cannot be further divided and have a duration of no more than one day. During task decomposition, don't worry about quantity, relationships or correctness. Simply list the tasks in a 'simple and rough' manner. Once you reach the point of exhaustion and frustration, then start considering categorization, logic and correctness. In this process, add or remove tasks as necessary. It's important to include not only software engineering and requirements-related tasks but also trivial matters like team logistics, procurement, sick leave, resignations and new hires, as these can all affect project progress.

Second, after task decomposition, the next step is time scheduling. Generally, the time plan should be listed according to the software engineering lifecycle stages, detailing the planned start and end times, expected start and end times, and actual start and end times for each task. Calculate the task duration based on the start and end times to serve as a basis for calculating workload and tracking plan completion rates. This comprehensive time plan is typically called a master plan.

In the master plan, phases and times are listed in columns, and tasks are listed in rows, forming a typical Gantt chart. The benefit of this arrangement is the clear visibility of each task's progress, the completion status of each phase, the overall project completion status and the progress of individual tasks, making it very suitable for tracking and guiding the project implementation process.

Third, based on the time plan, create a resource plan. Each task should be assigned to a responsible person. With the task duration and the number of people executing it, you can calculate the workload for each task. Summing up all tasks' workloads gives the project's total workload, which in turn determines the budget in person-months and monetary terms. Based on the time and personnel plans, you can quickly create a resource plan, outlining the resource entry and exit times, the number of days each person is needed, and identifying any resource conflicts or necessary adjustments.

With a resource plan, you can track resource usage. If there are deviations in resource usage, adjustments can be made according to the plan. By comparing the actual resource usage with the master plan's task schedule and execution status, you can clearly understand whether progress and resource input are aligned.

Fourth, in addition to the master plan and resource plan, create high-level and mid-level plans. The high-level plan outlines major milestones and progress and is often used in reports to senior management. Generally, high-level plans are presented in graphical form rather than tables.

The mid-level plan bridges the high-level plan and the master plan. It aggregates tasks by groups or major menu items, usually on a monthly cycle, and is primarily presented in tabular form. The goal is to clearly see the execution status of various major phases of the project.

Fifth, during project execution, each group leader needs to create detailed plans for their subgroup. This process involves breaking down the group's tasks into daily tasks for each member and summarizing the weekly tasks. This detailed plan is crucial for managing each person's tasks, ensuring that everyone follows the plan, and ultimately contributing to the project's timely completion.

Sixth, track the project's execution by recording actual performance in the master plan. Automatically calculate the completion percentage of each phase and monitor whether the project is on schedule or delayed, whether progress is faster or slower than resource input, whether there will be delays in the project timeline, and whether there are cost overruns. Add elements such as completion percentage, workload, task weight, importance and urgency to the master plan to control the project comprehensively.

When making plans, many people fall into some common pitfalls. For example, some managers always believe that the more detailed and complex the plan, the better. As a result, they end up writing a lengthy plan that overwhelms the most crucial content. When subordinates see such a plan, they feel confused and cannot clearly understand what they are supposed to do. How can they possibly execute it well? The simpler the plan, the easier it is to execute. Peter Drucker's story illustrates this point well.

When Peter Drucker was young, he worked at a bank in London. He wrote a restructuring plan and submitted it to his superior. The superior glanced at it and then said, "Alright, now let's call Louis in to take a look at your plan."

Drucker was surprised and said, "Louis is our company's youngest bookkeeper. He has no experience and, as you know, his performance is the worst in our company. What is the point of having him review this plan?"

The superior replied, "That's precisely my intention. If even Louis can easily understand your plan, then we can go ahead and execute it. If he finds it difficult to understand, the plan might be too complicated to be carried out. Whenever we do anything, we must consider whether a 'fool' can understand it – because, in the end, any task will ultimately be carried out by some 'fools.'"

Another common pitfall is that some managers create plans filled with vague jargon, leaving executors unsure of where to start. Even with repeated urging, they remain inactive. When making a plan, it's essential to avoid lofty slogans that nobody wants to hear. Be as specific as possible and directly tell the people executing the plan when and where they should do what and meet what standards.

ORGANIZATION IS THE SYSTEM OF DIVISION OF TASKS, RESPONSIBILITIES AND PROCESSES

The second function of management is organizing. Why establish an organization? Because **an organization is a responsibility system built around tasks or goals.** Goals and work tasks need to be assigned to specific individuals who are responsible for them to ensure final results. If everyone is in charge, it essentially means no one is responsible, leading to a loss of control over organizational goals.

There are two types of responsibility systems in organizations: simple and complex. A simple organization uses a very straightforward work distribution method, such as evenly distributing the same tasks to each person, which requires minimal management. This method is often referred to as the 'contract system.' In this model, tasks that can be measured with numerical indicators are broken down and assigned to each responsible person, who is then required to complete these indicators regularly. The incentives for the responsible individuals are directly tied to the completion of these numerical indicators. This type of management is very worry-free, but overall efficiency is not high. Why is that?

Because growth comes from efficiency, efficiency comes from specialization, specialization comes from long-term focus, and focus requires division of labor. A hallmark of modern enterprises is their ability to achieve large-scale specialized division of labor. In the automotive industry, Henry Ford was the first to implement the assembly line in his company, breaking down and dividing the work of assembling cars. As a result, Ford Motor Company experienced rapid growth, and the overall efficiency of the automotive industry saw a significant leap, fully demonstrating the value of the division of labor. The same principle applies to other sectors. Division of labor, combined with collaboration, is what we refer to as an organized enterprise; otherwise, it can only be called a 'small workshop.'

Some might argue that they already have a division of labor in place; for example, they don't have coders doing sales or accountants handling recruitment. Indeed, in a company, functions like research and development, sales, finance and human resources are distinct and require specialization, which is a widely accepted practice in the workplace. But what happens if we break it down further?

If we dissect the work of marketing, we find that the specific tasks are also diverse. Tasks such as sensing industry trends, acquiring business opportunities, bidding, financing and debt collection all require different personal capabilities and team skills. For instance, if someone who excels in writing proposals is tasked with debt collection, the outcome would likely be far from satisfactory.

The same principle applies to R&D work. Defining product features, writing code and negotiating with partners about product requirements all require different core competencies. In an R&D team, if we ask a developer who excels at coding according to fixed requirements to define a user experience that is centric to the consumer software product, the outcome is likely to be unsatisfactory. Although these tasks are all part of 'R&D work,' the required skills and underlying abilities are completely different. The former requires proficient coding skills, while the latter demands a deep understanding of user needs. It's rare to find both skills in the same individual.

In the early stages of business development, we might not have a clear understanding of the workflow for new business operations, making it difficult to establish a division of labor and responsibility system. During this phase, everyone works toward the overall goal, and there is often significant overlap and ambiguity between the roughly divided roles. This situation is acceptable and even encouraged. Many companies adopt a 'contract system' during their startup phase, following this approach. However, as the business gradually stabilizes and managers gain a better understanding of the business processes, if many employees are still juggling multiple roles, it indicates that managers have been lazy in establishing clear divisions of labor and responsibility systems. Without this, large-scale operations cannot be achieved, and the company will struggle to grow significantly or build long-term competitive capabilities.

A good manager must produce not only business results but also the 'organization' as a product. The core of this organizational product is clear processes, clear division of labor, clear responsibilities and clear structure. How can this series of 'clarifications' be implemented? The key is to execute them at each specific 'key position.'

Once the work processes are clear, we can analyse which tasks are important and what kinds of positions need to be designed, matching them with individuals who have the required skills to complete these tasks. Our analysis forms our definition of key positions. After defining these key positions, we find people who possess the necessary abilities, establish incentive policies for completing key tasks, and place the right people in the right positions with appropriate incentives, thus ensuring that the business system operates smoothly. Ultimately, the organization will take shape in a specific structure, where each node has its corresponding responsibility system.

Therefore, to evaluate whether someone's management work is successful, we need to see if they have established the responsibility system and structure of the organization.

Of course, the creation of the 'organization' as a product cannot be achieved overnight; it requires continuous refinement. In the early stages of business exploration, we can establish agile teams to explore initial divisions of labor. As the business continues to develop and external circumstances change, the organization evolves and grows. For example, Ford Motor Company initially established the assembly line. As the organization grew larger, it added multiple workshops and factories, forming large offices and even alliances with various enterprises. Throughout this ongoing process of change and evolution, managers must consistently focus on and continually refine the 'organization' product rather than letting it develop unchecked.

In the process of organizational development, people from different companies and organizational cultures come together to communicate and collaborate, which often leads to conflicts and disagreements. At this point, the third function of management – coordinating – becomes essential.

COORDINATION MAKES CONFLICTS DISAPPEAR UNNOTICED

One of the primary responsibilities of a manager is decision-making, which often involves dealing with both certain and uncertain situations. When facing uncertainty, conflicts and disagreements are likely to arise whenever two or more people are involved. Resolving these conflicts relies heavily on the manager's ability to coordinate. Coordination includes both internal and external aspects of the enterprise, and managers must coordinate tasks they lead as well as contribute to coordination in tasks led by others.

In the previous sections, we discussed the planning and organizing functions of management. When it comes to coordination, we also need to consider: What exactly is coordination? There are various answers to this question. Some say that coordination is the matching of resources within or across organizational structures. Others believe that coordination is about satisfying and controlling the interests, rights and responsibilities of all parties to achieve a common goal. There is also an additional view that coordination involves mobilizing all productive relationships and productivity within the existing structure and responsibility system to achieve the best possible results.

All these answers make sense, but they each view coordination from a partial perspective. To avoid the error of taking a narrow view of any concept, it's essential to consider its essence and key points. **Essentially, coordination is the communicative action of resolving conflicts to achieve a goal.**

When focusing on internal organization, we often find that coordination typically arises in areas without established rules and processes and from uncertain relationships. Before things are clarified and consensus is reached, managers need to coordinate and negotiate each detail individually. This process consumes a significant amount of time and energy, leading to very low work efficiency. To avoid such unnecessary internal friction, we should strive to transform uncertain relationships into certain ones.

Therefore, the real effort in coordination lies in continuously optimizing the responsibility system and processes, clarifying various relationships, and resolving uncertain issues upfront. It is much simpler to communicate and reach consensus on processes and the responsibility system in advance than to address each conflict in detail. By following established processes when issues arise, not only will managers find their work easier, but the overall efficiency of the organization will also improve.

In the early development of Digital China's distribution business, the group maintained a relatively loose management approach for newly signed product lines. This loose management led to the possibility of some new product lines not meeting development expectations, making it difficult to recover early personnel and financial investments and even resulting in excess inventory that could jeopardize operations.

To address this issue, the group began to control the new product signing process strictly. In addition to the original approval from the business general manager, the risk management department, finance department and business development department were also involved in the approval process. While this approach helped control risk, it introduced new problems. Since each department had different concerns, the business manager had to explain the same issue four times, often leading to multiple rounds of back-and-forth discussions. As a result, the signing process could be delayed by up to two months, hindering business development.

To strike a balance between efficiency and risk, the product management department initiated internal coordination.

First, they collaborated with relevant departments, including business line managers, the risk management department, the finance department, and the business development department,

to jointly develop evaluation criteria for introducing new product lines.
1. Products and technologies strongly aligned with the group's strategic development, ensuring minimal execution risk, could be introduced with lenient requirements.
2. For products not strongly aligned with the group's strategic development, they must meet all the following conditions to be approved: annual revenue forecast of at least xx million RMB, with a three-year growth rate exceeding the group average; projected gross margin and net margin not lower than the average for similar businesses; return on investment not less than xx%; and no significant risk clauses in the agreement that cannot be borne.

Second, they established a New Product Project Review Committee to conduct multi-departmental, one-stop joint reviews. With complete documentation and fulfilment of conditions, the review time could be compressed to one or two hours. Even if a project is rejected during the process, having clear evaluation criteria means the project initiator is more likely to accept the rejection gracefully.

By establishing clear evaluation criteria and reshaping the review process, the signing of new products was effectively managed. This move not only improved internal decision-making efficiency but also considered the company's operational risks.

In addition to internal coordination, we often face the need for cross-organizational coordination, which typically involves aligning the goals of both organizations to achieve mutual benefits. 'Customer-centricity' is not just a slogan; it is fundamental to a company's survival and success. Only by being customer-centric – aligning the company's goals with those of the customers and creating value for them – can a company's value be realized, leading to profitability. In other words, making money is the result, not the cause.

When coordinating, we often find that conflicts in demands arise due to information asymmetry. Everyone has limitations in knowledge,

information, experience and capabilities, as well as diverse values and goals. Often, within their areas of authority, the parties involved seek to be scientifically informed yet are bounded by rational decisions.[9] Bounded rationality is a concept that lies between complete rationality and irrationality, and it manifests in the following ways:
- Inability to identify all alternative options.
- Inability to fully predict the consequences of all alternative options.
- Lacking a clear and completely consistent preference system to choose the optimal decision in various decision-making environments.

Coordination aims to address these issues by facilitating multidirectional communication, making asymmetric information as symmetric as possible for all parties involved, helping broaden their limited perspectives and encouraging the pursuit of common goals. The objective is to align the bounded rational decisions of all parties into a consensus that covers a wider range of considerations.

The adjustment of the organizational structure of the Middle Platform in Digital China fully illustrates this point.

Digital China's distribution business was established during the influx of overseas IT brands into China. As the China regional general agent for many overseas brands, Digital China has built an organizational structure centred around product manufacturers since its inception. It operates with business units as independent entities focused on serving these manufacturers and managing sales channels. Each business unit's operational strategy largely aligns with the respective manufacturer's strategies, aiming to implement marketing strategies in coordination with the manufacturers. To facilitate independent operations, besides sales personnel, the business units also employ functional staff responsible for business support roles. In the early stages, this operational management concept, similar to the 'Amoeba operating' model, helped the teams focus on business objectives and achieve excellent performance.

However, in recent years, with the increase in product categories and manufacturers and intensified market competition, the horizontal expansion of product categories has led to structural growth. This development has posed significant challenges to the business unit structure of Digital China, where disparities in the supply and demand of functional personnel across business units and overall inefficiency have become increasingly prominent. Some departments experiencing declining performance have resorted to laying off talented functional staff rather than reallocating them to new business units with faster growth and personnel needs under pressure to control costs, resulting in a significant waste of human resources. Starting in 2019, to address these issues, the company formulated an organizational transformation plan to establish an agile middle platform system. This middle platform system aims to be staffed primarily by functional personnel from various business units. By integrating functional personnel from each business unit and implementing a specialized division of labor, the company seeks to reuse personnel capabilities effectively, thereby enhancing the overall support efficiency for front-end operations across the organization.

After setting the goals for organizational transformation, a variety of issues arose: What is a 'middle platform'? Why is there a need to integrate functional personnel? What benefits can a new middle platform bring to each business unit? Why centralize all assistants from business units to the middle platform? How do we manage 'information security' with all assistants together? What if upstream suppliers are reluctant to share assistants with other brand suppliers? Isn't grouping a large number of people just 'putting old wine in a new bottle'? Besides continuing to support business operations, what else can consolidating our assistants achieve? What new responsibilities will the consolidated personnel in the middle platform have? Where is the strategic direction of the middle platform headed?

For a time, the business units involved in the transformation underwent significant atmospheric changes. Various emotions, such as suspicion, mistrust and worry, quickly spread. The integration of functional personnel faced numerous challenges.

Summarizing the difficulties and concerns, we find they mainly manifest in the following aspects.

1. Employees generally do not understand why functional personnel from various business units are being integrated into the middle platform, and some even perceive it as a cost-cutting measure by the company. Most are adopting a wait-and-see attitude or spreading negative sentiments – this is an issue at the 'why' level.
2. There is uncertainty about how such a large-scale integration of functional personnel should be carried out while ensuring operational continuity. How can the middle platform be effectively established? This pertains to the 'how to do' level.
3. The relationship between integrating functional personnel and establishing the middle platform is unclear. There is a lack of clarity among management regarding their understanding of the middle platform and the path to its implementation. At a smaller scale, consensus has not been reached. It represents a consensus-level issue within the organization.
4. Frontline employees are uncertain, leading to unstable work emotions and staff turnover, exacerbating suspicions and misunderstandings within the business departments; this affects team morale.
5. Determining new roles and responsibilities for the integrated personnel in the new middle platform has become a prominent concern that needs organizational management attention.

To address these problems, it is crucial to establish consensus among personnel from top to bottom. To achieve this, the company has initiated extensive organizational and coordinated communication efforts.

First, the executive committee has established a Functional Integration Task Force to oversee the integration plan of middle platform personnel, conducting monthly and biweekly meetings for collective decision-making on major issues.

Second, the middle platform has set up an operations management department and established a middle platform Integration

Project Team, concurrently launching a middle platform Process Simplification Project Group. This initiative revolves around optimizing critical business processes in collaboration with various business units, seeking consensus beyond sensitive personnel integration, and actively seeking points of synergy with business units.

Third, starting with pressure on business units that are struggling with performance (due to the lack of strong willingness for change among departments with relatively good performance), individual communications with general managers or operations directors of business units address the 'pain points' faced by business departments. This approach utilizes business plan communications, combined with profit-and-loss analysis of expenditure structures, guiding business units to acknowledge the group-level establishment of the middle platform's original intention, thereby accepting the concept of a 'shared operation team.'

Fourth, apart from seeking consensus from vertical business departments, efforts are initiated from horizontal area platforms, selecting branch[10] managers with strong reform intentions to discuss and assess the feasibility of integrating regional platform personnel.

Fifth, proactively 'going out,' directors from headquarters visit various regional branches, engaging with grassroots employees and frontline sales teams, addressing issues and listening to feedback to dispel concerns. In the latter half of 2019 alone, committee members visited all national branches, requiring directors and branch managers to spend at least 50% of their time interacting with frontline employees through discussions and seminars. This work has become a pivotal stage in the core activities of the middle platform backbone.

Through multiple rounds of multidimensional communication, coordination and adjustment, the functional personnel of the business units have begun to transition structurally toward the middle platform. Initial consensus has been reached on functional integration, and organizational coordination efforts are showing initial effectiveness. Doing so has laid a solid foundation for setting clear goals, devising pathways and piloting implementation in subsequent stages. During this transformation process, a group of motivated and capable leaders has also emerged, ready to take on greater responsibilities in driving the group's transformation.

Looking back at the implementation process of this organizational transformation shows that it involved a wide range of personnel, multiple objectives and high complexity. The transformation aimed not only to improve the productivity of the entire company's functional personnel but also to ensure the continuous smooth operation of the business while discovering excellent talent for the company's future development. Multiple goals needed to be balanced simultaneously. During this period, strategic guidance, grassroots engagement, iterative experimentation and bold reforms were essential. Each transformational step required extensive coordination to ensure consensus among relevant stakeholders. This coordination has been a key factor contributing to the success of this transformation and serves as a valuable lesson for future endeavors.

In the process of coordination, it's essential to handle the persuasion work, which is an art form in itself. From my perspective, to effectively coordinate, one typically needs to engage in at least three rounds of persuasion work: first, understand what the other party is thinking; second, express your thoughts and observe the other party's reaction; and only on the third attempt might the other party be persuaded. It's difficult to convince someone right from the start; it requires a process.

The process of coordination must recognize that everything we do should seek truth and adhere to reality. Only truth can prevail over everything else, not based on who speaks the loudest or who is most adept at citing sources, but through practical verification that proves it correct, leading everyone to consensus. In this process of understanding and practice, we need to set aside personal pride, engage in criticism and self-criticism, and adopt democratic methods to discover the truth collectively and put it into practice.

ACHIEVING CONTROL RELIES ON IDENTIFYING KEY VARIABLES

Management is a practice, and its essence lies not in knowledge but in action. Control is an indispensable link to achieving our desired goals through action and discovering and resolving issues in action. When we talk about control, we are not focusing on specific 'individuals' or specific 'events' but rather on a system.

All systems have two states: input and output. When we are unfamiliar with the internal workings of a system, we can only observe that we input condition A into the system and eventually obtain result B. The internal workings of the system are like a black box to us – we do not know how A evolves into B. In other words, without understanding the system's rules, we cannot predict or control result B. In many management processes, the aim is to achieve controllable results. However, if the goals are set but the results are uncontrollable, then regardless of whether the goals are achieved, management is ineffective.

To achieve controllability in enterprise management, the core is to achieve 'getting the desired output B by changing the input A.' How can this be achieved? Cybernetics provides a straightforward logic: We need to identify the control variables in the system. By adjusting and transforming these control variables, we can ensure that the system's output meets our expectations. This process involves a continuous cycle of discovering, inspecting, adjusting, verifying and readjusting the control variables. It gradually transforms the operational mechanism of the system from unknown to known, and it clarifies the ongoing tasks of management.

In our daily management processes, it's crucial to reflect often: Have we truly achieved control? Have we identified and managed the key variables? Are we confident in understanding the results and goals, or are we merely hoping for good luck? Whether it's producing financial statements, applying for qualifications for new business units or managing projects, our work involves identifying control variables to achieve control over outcomes.

Our management of a particular affair is akin to running a loop in a computer programming language. The output state is verified; if 'yes,' it proceeds to the next process, and if 'no,' it loops back to start. Effective control means that after verifying 'no,' adjusting the input control variables ensures that the program's outcome turns into 'yes.'

Program execution takes time, just as completing tasks in a business requires time, and achieving goals is also time-bound. Therefore, our adjustments to control variables need to be more precise and efficient. At the same time, when transitioning from a single goal to multiple goals, the factors involved increase, making the discovery and adjustment of control variables more complex. This complexity often exceeds the limits of our brain's information storage capacity. Addressing these issues requires our management approach to shift from empiricism to data-driven strategies.

Digital China has conducted extensive exploration and practical initiatives in data-driven strategies, which could potentially offer valuable insights for managers.

In 2019, following the implementation of the middle platform strategy, Digital China began unified management of operational personnel across its various business units. During this period, significant issues were identified in data analysis across different levels and departments. These issues included redundant data processing, frequent errors in manual data handling and inconsistencies in data standards, all of which severely impacted operational efficiency. Additionally, personalized data processing and analysis tasks were scattered across different operational teams within each business unit. These tasks varied in methods and presentation, with no unified storage system for files. As a result, a substantial amount of data assets was at risk of being lost as personnel moved within the company, preventing the accumulation of corporate data assets.

To enhance overall operational management efficiency, the middle platform initiated a 'Data Visualization' project. The goal is to unify the processing and presentation of operational data using visualization tools, ensuring consistency in data standards, reducing manual intervention and enabling real-time display.

After a year of implementation, by the end of 2019, the project had made some progress. Business operational data was systematically displayed across various dimensions, and the system achieved the following functionalities:

Hierarchical access: A set of reports is made accessible through permission allocation for personnel at different levels and departments.

Real-time and dynamic: Data directly integrated from data warehouses and ERP systems, displaying results in real-time and dynamically without the need for manual processing by analysts.

Aggregation: Reports of all categories are consolidated into a single platform, eliminating the need to open multiple reports or files.

Customization: Business analysts can request customized visualizations tailored to their specific business management needs from the project team.

After another year of system operation, by the end of 2020, the visualization system had attracted hundreds of operational management personnel to become active users.

In early 2021, as the entire industry elevated 'digital transformation' to unprecedented heights, the company also realized the imperative of data-driven operational transformation. Consequently, the data visualization project team was upgraded to the data operations department, tasked with handling data-related work for the company's digital middle platform in a more specialized manner.

Using a Business Intelligence (BI)[11] system to present data analysis results and visualization dashboards, ultimately supporting users' business decisions, is the ultimate goal of data visualization construction. To achieve this goal, the data operations team needs to provide clean, accurate and comprehensive data sources to ensure the value of the data presented to users. Additionally, it is necessary to continuously unearth users' needs, shifting from traditional management reporting to supporting decision-making scenarios and data modelling. Numerous challenges have been encountered during the project's progress, with the following being the most significant:

1) Mindset issues: There is inertia in traditional empirical thinking, with resistance or lack of understanding toward data-driven work methods.
2) Data issues: Existing data quality and quantity do not meet the system's requirements.
3) Talent issues: The composition and allocation of resources within the central operations analysis team are still traditional, with inadequate investment and competence in systematic data analysis.
4) Mechanism issues: Data-driven operational work involves replacing habits and patterns, making it difficult to define specific work outcomes and thereby hindering progress.

To address these issues, the data operations team actively pursued a series of initiatives for the data visualization system through strategic guidance, talent acquisition, a user-centric approach and a balanced focus on development and operations.

In-depth user engagement: From the initial system content research, users are deeply involved in the development and design process. The data operations team keeps users updated on the latest system content through regular short videos and training sessions. After the content goes live, user feedback is collected regularly to adjust and iterate the content promptly.

From addition to subtraction: In the early stages of system development, to encourage the formation of usage habits and the development of interest, an approach of accepting all user demands was adopted, continuously adding content. However, after reaching a certain stage of content development, a lot of repetitive and low-value work began to appear, leading to system overload and wastage of development resources. The data operations team then shifted their strategy from addition to subtraction, proactively reducing the schedule for project content development. They conducted in-depth reviews and guidance on personalized requests and implemented strict quality control for each piece of content launched, moving away from pursuing quantity over quality.

Initiating data governance: As the scope of visualization expanded beyond operational data to include business opportunities, contracts, processes and other diverse data categories, the quality issues with data sources became increasingly prominent. Inaccurate and unclean data could harm rather than add value to business decisions. Therefore, the work of master data governance was prioritized, presenting the data operations team with even higher challenges.

After a year of effort, by the end of 2021, the system's registered users had essentially encompassed all personnel that the system could cover, with active users accounting for nearly 50%.

After more than two years of practice, an increasing number of people have developed the habit of using the visualization system. Logging in and using the system daily has become an important part of everyone's routine work. Operational staff are handling data manually less and less. In routine work and regular meetings, data analysis and business reporting can be directly extracted from the system, or the system can be used to conduct communication or presentation sessions directly. The system's focus on user personalization needs has also increased, providing not only department-specific and professional dimension data analyses but also personalized dashboards tailored to different roles. Whether it's business unit leaders or frontline sales personnel, everyone can use the system to monitor their relevant business performance in real time.

The work of transforming operations to be data-driven is just one aspect of business analysis management. It involves digitalizing touchpoints, bringing business processes online and visualizing data across front, middle and back-office departments.

This approach enables digital transformation across the entire business value chain, supporting data visualization and decision-making. Whether it's business leaders, product managers, sales teams or the marketing, human resources and finance departments, all can leverage the power of data for more efficient management and decision-making and thus benefit from it.

The essence of data-driven operations is to support decision-making, ultimately aiming to enhance efficiency, reduce costs and promote growth. In our daily work, we can see that decision-making scenarios vary significantly from person to person. Actually, the differences in decisions made by different individuals are primarily influenced by two factors: One is the variety of input background information, and the other is different decision-making principles. The amount and quality of background information data can affect decision-making; similarly, different decision-making principles can influence specific decision choices.

In aiming to employ data-driven operations, we essentially focus on two key objectives. First, we strive to standardize the background data that influences decisions, unifying standards and definitions to ensure that all decision-makers have access to the highest quality data. Second, by continuously tracking business processes, we seek to identify and extract excellent decision-making principles, which are then codified into system algorithms and models. Through these efforts, the decision-making process that traditionally relied heavily on human experience is divided into two parts: One part involves simple, repeatable tasks executed by algorithms, and the other, more complex part, utilizes data and business process tracking to enable managers to quantify, track, calibrate and fine-tune decisions.

It is undeniable that in many mature business sectors, empiricism remains a very economical option. However, when massive changes across the industry are inevitable and cross-industry business decisions are necessary, I hope that data-driven approaches will become a useful and convenient tool for managers to employ effectively.

CHAPTER 3

THE RIGHT APPROACH TO TIME MANAGEMENT DOUBLES EFFECTIVENESS

MAKE GOOD USE OF EFFECTIVE TIME MANAGEMENT TOOLS

After reevaluating time management from a managerial perspective, I believe that more and more people are eagerly seeking answers to the question of 'how to manage time effectively.' In fact, time management is not difficult; the key lies in making good use of effective time management methods and tools. As the ancient saying goes, "To do a good job, one must first sharpen one's tools."

Good time management methods and tools can help us improve the accuracy of our judgements and the efficiency of our decision-making. At this point, many people may wonder: What does time management have to do with decision-making? In fact, there is a deep and intricate connection between the two.

The internal and external environments that enterprises face are filled with uncertainties, requiring managers to make frequent decisions. Accurate judgement means that managers have a good understanding of the company's situation, the external environment or the status of competitors, enabling them to make wise choices or decisions.

If we look at MBA management courses, we can see that the business administration education model is mostly structured as follows: First, it builds managers' confidence in their instincts and intuition, enabling them to make accurate judgements instantly. Then, through extensive case studies and other examples, it trains managers in making informed judgements.

However, extensive research has found that human judgement is often inaccurate, and people frequently lack awareness of their inaccurate judgements. Therefore, in enterprises, it is not uncommon for managers to be overconfident and overestimate their decision-making abilities. MIT scientist Andrew McAfee stated, "There is a rationale for humans to trust their intuition, but intuition is often wrong. In the Second Machine Age, a simple rule applies: as the volume of data increases, the importance of human judgement should decrease."

This inaccuracy in judgement often occurs in enterprises. For example, at Digital China, some managers and employees, despite having learned many time management methods, do not apply them in their actual work. Some say that they have already listed the important tasks, so there's no need to list the unimportant ones. Others claim that even though they haven't used a specific tool, they have incorporated the method into their thinking process. They prefer to trust their judgement rather than rely on scientific methods.

Therefore, managers should not simply trust their judgement. Confidence is beneficial, but overconfidence can lead to negative outcomes. Among the many factors influencing managers to make the right judgements and decisions, practical experience and thinking patterns are crucial internal factors. In contrast, the difficulty and complexity of decisions are external factors. Judging the content and difficulty of a task may seem straightforward, but without careful consideration, the results can still be erroneous.

By using time management methods and tools to prioritize and organize the information and data we have, we can deeply analyse our current situation. In this process, we often discover discrepancies between what we 'thought' and what the 'reality' is. This discovery leads to a clearer and deeper understanding of our work, resulting in more reasonable and accurate judgements and decisions.

However, with the myriad time management methods and tools available, which ones are truly effective and practical? In fact, the correct approaches often adhere to fundamental principles. Overly flashy methods may either have limited usefulness or be difficult to maintain consistently.

Here are seven basic time management skills that I recommend practising consistently over the long term:
- List everything: Write down all tasks and activities.
- Identify priorities: Identify the important tasks from the list.

- Fill the four quadrants: Categorize tasks using the Eisenhower Matrix by adding urgency to the importance dimension, creating a two-dimensional chart.
- Create a schedule: Organize all tasks within a timeline.
- Write weekly reports: Summarize and review weekly work, ensuring key points are highlighted.
- Delegate: Delegate controllable tasks to subordinates.
- Reflect and summarize: Regularly review and reflect on progress, conducting timely reviews.

LEARN HOW TO 'LIST EVERYTHING'

In 2001, shortly after its establishment, Digital China held its first IPO roadshow. The schedule was extremely tight, with even meal and restroom breaks strictly controlled. During this time, a fund manager suddenly made two very demanding requests: first, to dismiss the investment banking personnel responsible for on-site coordination and presentations, insisting on direct discussions between our side and theirs since our cooperation had no substantive relation with the investment bank; second, to discard the extensive preparatory materials, as pre-prepared information could be misleading, and only extemporaneous presentations would be convincing.

Faced with such a challenging situation, how could we persuade the investors and gain their trust and approval? It was the habit of listing everything that helped us. I asked my colleagues to bring a whiteboard, and as I spoke, I started listing the key points. The investors were immediately impressed. Later, someone told me that it was this simple habit that made them realize that this would be a very practical and systematic collaboration.

Listing everything is a fundamental yet highly effective time management tool. Simply put, it involves listing out your thoughts and ideas.

Don't underestimate the process of putting your thoughts on paper. Many people think they have a lot of content in their minds, but they don't realize that this content is often a tangled mess. By listing everything, you can gradually clarify and structure the thoughts in your mind. Therefore, the first function of listing everything is to help us organize our thoughts.

The second function is to achieve consensus. Communication within a team is different from one-on-one interactions. Managers who excel at one-on-one communication may not necessarily be good at team communication. When senior leaders at Digital China are researching a task or formulating a policy, they often gather team members together and have each person list five key tasks, which are then compiled into a comprehensive list.

During this listing process, team members often realize that they have only a superficial understanding of others' work and even their own work. Listing everything is a process of clarification, helping to understand what everyone truly thinks about the issue. By listing the key points, discussing them, and refining the list, a consensus is eventually formed, which is an essential part of team building.

Listing everything also has another function: it greatly improves time utilization. By listing everything that needs to be done each week and each month and placing these tasks in the 'four quadrants' (which will be discussed next), you can determine which tasks should be done, which should not be done, or which should continue to be done. This practice significantly increases time utilization efficiency.

At this point, many people may still be unclear about how to 'list everything.' Let's take a look at how a subsidiary of DCITS used this method to advance its intern recruitment management. Through this case study, you can gain a more intuitive understanding of the process of listing everything.

A subsidiary of DCITS has a tradition of recruiting interns to build up their technical team reserves. In the first quarter of 2021, the team faced dual challenges from their business demands and the COVID-19 pandemic, significantly impacting the intern recruitment process. To address this, the head of human resources held a discussion meeting where each department used the listing everything method to identify and list the key issues they believed needed to be addressed.

1. What internship opportunities can we create for interns this year, and when should they be introduced? – service delivery department
2. Is it better to have more sources of interns in the current market environment? – business department
3. How can we deepen the collaboration with our current partner universities? – human resources department
4. How can we better retain the outstanding interns of the 2021 cohort? – business department
5. Does the intern training and mentorship program need to be iterated and upgraded for 2021? – business department, human resources department
6. How can we improve the skill levels of interns during peak project periods? – business department, service delivery department
7. What are the improvement plans for enhancing intern compensation and benefits? – business department, human resources department
8. How should the interns recruited by the R&D base and business units be allocated? – R&D base
9. How can we accelerate the interns' understanding of the industry and the company to promote stability? – human resources department
10. How can we ensure business compliance when employing interns? – product line
11. How can the business units coordinate to carry out university-enterprise cooperation and provide pre-job training for interns? – service delivery department, human resources department, business department
12. Do the KPI indicators for interns in each business unit need to be revised? – business department, human resources department
13. How can we determine the phase-wise acceptance criteria for intern work? – business department, human resources department

Through this open exchange meeting, the business and support departments used the listing everything method to review the issues encountered in the current intern recruitment process. They combined these issues with the 'four quadrants' methodology to prioritize them, ultimately identifying two key areas for improvement to address the challenges in recruiting interns.

1. Sources of intern recruitment: Addressing the current issue of numerous and inconsistent university-enterprise collaborations.
2. Intern empowerment and training: Ensuring that training and empowerment align with the year's project peak periods.

With improvements to these two areas of consensus, the introduction of interns has become significantly more effective.

In daily work, if all teams use this method to reach consensus – such as determining how to break down key tasks for each year and each quarter or setting the team's development direction – team members will likely find it easier to accept compared to directly assigning tasks. Consequently, the execution will be more effective.

Why does this happen? Because in most cases, a person can only do something well if they genuinely agree with it. Just as Newton often forgot to eat and sleep while studying physics, and Beethoven would become utterly absorbed when playing the piano, people need to be genuinely willing to do something imaginative and creative and persist over the long term. In the process of team building, continually listing everything and reaching consensus helps ensure that team members genuinely recognize and agree with the tasks, fostering commitment and sustained effort.

To effectively 'list everything,' we can use simple and effective tools, such as mind maps (see Figure 3-1). Mind maps, also known as concept maps or tree diagrams, are so-called because their creation process simulates the thinking process of the human brain. Human thinking is divergent, allowing us to associate a keyword with other words and concepts, continually generating related content. The formation of a mind map follows this process of continuous divergence based on a central theme. By drawing lines to list associated concepts and ideas and representing them according to certain hierarchical or subordinate relationships, our understanding of the central theme becomes increasingly comprehensive.

FIGURE 3-1

EXAMPLE OF A MIND MAP FOR LISTING EVERYTHING DURING A PHASE DISCUSSION MEETING FOR A BUSINESS

A mind map can be drawn directly on a whiteboard or paper or created using software. Nowadays, there are many mind-mapping software options available to us. In addition to drawing mind maps, they can also be exported as images or PDF files for archiving and communication. We can choose the tool based on the work scenario.

Today, listing everything has become a habit not just for me but for all employees at Digital China. In Digital China's office building, each meeting room is equipped with a large glass whiteboard that covers an entire wall, along with markers and erasers. This setup is designed so that teams can continually 'list everything' during meetings, promptly reach a consensus and avoid wasting time. The whiteboards in every meeting room are filled with words and various diagrams, which, in my view, are far more aesthetically pleasing than decorative paintings.

At the end of 2018, when Digital China's cloud workgroup was formulating the 2019 cloud work plan and discussing the development of cloud solutions, everyone listed all of Digital China's solutions on the whiteboard. They identified which solutions were in the lab stage, which had client cases and which aligned better with future technology trends. By first brainstorming and listing everything, then grouping similar items based on different dimensions and actual conditions, the team quickly developed executable rules and plans, even clarifying responsibilities and divisions of labor.

In fact, not just solutions but many ideas and strategies at Digital China have been clarified and enriched bit by bit using this approach. Through this method, the team has been able to find methods, develop strategies and reach consensus during the process.

IDENTIFY THE MOST IMPORTANT 20%

After mastering the listing everything method, the next step in time management is to determine the importance of each 'item.' In most cases, the most important items typically won't exceed 20% of the total. This concept is based on an important management principle known as the Pareto Principle or the 80/20 Rule.

Whether in life or at work, we often see people who are constantly busy with various tasks, appearing to be highly capable. However, in the end, we find that these individuals have not accomplished much. In contrast, some people who may not seem exceptionally smart achieve significant success because they focus intensely and diligently on doing one thing well. Why does this happen? It is because they, like a staple, concentrate on the most important task without hesitation or wavering, persisting until the end.

In everyday life, we often use a stapler. Even the sharpest knife would struggle to cut through a stack of dozens or hundreds of sheets of paper all at once. Yet, the seemingly insignificant staple can bind them securely in an instant. The reason lies in the fact that the staple focuses all its force on two concentrated points.

That is the principle that the 80/20 Rule teaches us: We can create the greatest value by focusing time and energy on a few key tasks.

The 80/20 Rule – also known as the Pareto Principle, the Law of the Vital Few, the Principle of Least Effort, the Principle of Imbalance, the Jewish Law and the Matley Principle – was first proposed by Italian economist and sociologist Vilfredo Pareto in the late 19th century.

He pointed out that in any specific group, the important factors usually constitute a minority, while the unimportant factors make up the majority. Therefore, by focusing on controlling a few vital factors, one can effectively command the overall situation.

In 1897, Pareto developed a keen interest in the patterns of wealth and income among the British population and conducted a year-long study on this topic. Through careful observation and investigation, he discovered a phenomenon: The majority of wealth in society was controlled by a small number of people. Moreover, there was a subtle relationship between the percentage of a specific group in the total population and the share of total income they held. Ultimately, he concluded that 20% of the people in society held 80% of the wealth, indicating that wealth distribution among the population was imbalanced.

In 1941, a management consultant named Joseph Juran applied Pareto's research findings to quality issues and discovered that the 80/20 Rule indeed had universal applicability. He found that 80% of quality problems were caused by 20% of the issues, a phenomenon he referred to as the 'vital few and trivial many,' also known as the Pareto Principle or the 80/20 Rule.

There are multiple interpretations of the 80/20 Rule in economics, with three particularly noteworthy explanations. First, wealth distribution: 20% of the wealthy people own 80% of the world's wealth, while the remaining 80% of the population share 20% of the wealth. Second, effort and results: 80% of the results in work come from 20% of the effort, while 80% of the effort yields only 20% of the results. Third, profit distribution: 80% of profits come from 20% of the important clients, while the remaining 20% of profits come from 80% of the regular clients. The majority, 80%, only causes a minor impact, whereas the minority, 20%, has a major, significant influence. Therefore, the 'vital few' are what we should focus on the most. For example, when designing a product brochure, the most important elements are clearly stating the product name, price, specifications and contact information. These key pieces of information may occupy only a small portion of the brochure, but their impact is substantial. Without clear information, no matter how beautiful your images are, others will not know what the product is or how to purchase it.

When managing time, we should follow the same principle – we should focus 80% of our time on the 20% of core tasks. Similarly, by concentrating on the small 20% of tasks that have a significant impact, we can solve 80% of the problems. Completing this crucial 20% can improve work efficiency more than the remaining 80% of tasks combined. Conversely, if this 20% of work is not done well or contains errors, the consequences will be much more severe than mistakes in other tasks. Traditional culture also holds similar views. As stated in "The Great Learning," from *The Book of Rites* (Daxue): "Things have their roots and branches, affairs have their beginnings and ends. To know what comes first and what comes last is to approach the Way."[12] In modern terms, this means 'prioritize important tasks.'

Prioritizing important tasks is crucial in your work. No matter what you do, you must first identify the most important 20% of tasks to achieve greater efficiency and effectiveness.

One of my subordinates was recently promoted to general manager of a business unit, and he found himself overwhelmed with a multitude of tasks. At first, he was so busy every day that he was distressed. One day, he met me and shook his head repeatedly, saying, "I've wasted a lot of time, and I've accomplished nothing."

I told him, "Your fundamental problem is that you haven't been focusing your time on the most critical tasks." I then asked him to answer a few questions.

1. Do you know what the most important tasks in your work are?
2. Where do you spend most of your time?
3. Which tasks yield the most significant results?

He spent an entire day reflecting on his work and realized that, for a manager, the most important goal is to establish and maintain a good management system. He recognized that many of his tasks were in service of this goal. He categorized his work, deciding which tasks could be delegated to others and which had to be handled personally. He prioritized the tasks that required his direct attention. By organizing his work in this way, he could focus most of his time on the core task of building the management system. Doing so allowed him to concentrate on one primary task while others could handle issues in different areas without taking up his time.

After implementing this method for a while, his work efficiency improved significantly.

Of course, the remaining 80% of tasks are not unimportant. Ideally, people would like to handle everything perfectly. However, a person's energy is limited and continuously depletes throughout the day. Therefore, focusing primarily on the 20% of more important tasks is a necessary compromise, making 'priority to important tasks' an unavoidable strategy.

Everyone is surrounded by various tasks from work and life every day, and handling most of these tasks requires willpower. According to the 'ego depletion' theory, each task depletes a bit of a person's energy and execution capacity. When there are many trivial tasks, the important ones that require a lot of energy tend to get buried. As a result, people often find themselves acting like firefighters, constantly busy but never addressing the most critical issues.

Therefore, the 80/20 Rule in time management suggests that people should not strive to do as many things as possible but rather set limits for themselves to focus on the most important tasks. As the management guru Peter Drucker once said, "If there is any one 'secret' in effectiveness, it is concentration. Effective executives do first things first, and they do one thing at a time." Continuously refining the criteria for identifying the 'important 20%' is a crucial task for managers in practical work.

Generally speaking, these are the criteria for making these judgements:
- Key tasks for implementing the company's strategy
- Tasks that can bring significant returns to the business
- Tasks with major risks
- Tasks with a compounding effect
- Tasks with leverage effects

The principles mentioned above provide relatively coarse granularity. In practice, due to differences in the nature of the business, key tasks can vary significantly. Specifically, when dealing with particular business scenarios, a reasonable assessment requires considering three aspects: industry, specialization and technology. It's essential to avoid making blanket statements.

PRIORITIZE TASKS WITH QUADRANTS

In addition to the 80/20 Rule, it is crucial to apply a more advanced tool known as the Four Quadrants Method, also called the Eisenhower Matrix.

The Four Quadrants Method is a time management theory proposed by American management guru Stephen Covey. It is a specialized method for managing time. The Four Quadrants Method sorts tasks based on two criteria: importance and urgency. Importance is represented on the vertical axis, and urgency is shown on the horizontal axis, forming four quadrants (see Figure 3-2).

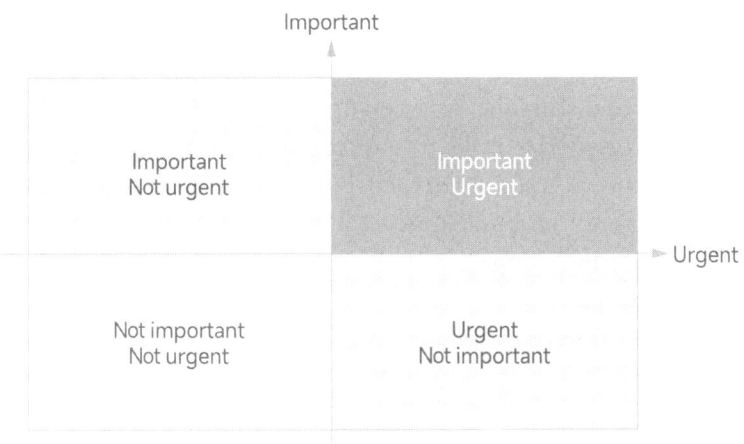

FIGURE 3-2
TIME MANAGEMENT FOUR QUADRANTS

- Quadrant I: important and urgent tasks. For example, visiting important clients, addressing project delivery risks, resolving system failures and dealing with delivery obstacles.
- Quadrant II: important but not urgent tasks. For example, strategic planning, technology research, talent development and knowledge management.
- Quadrant III: urgent but not important tasks. For example, responding to emails, approving routine business processes, attending regular meetings, making and receiving phone calls and meeting unexpected visitors.
- Quadrant IV: not important and not urgent tasks. For example, unproductive socializing and attending irrelevant meetings.

Obviously, to realize the value of life, one should focus one's energy on important tasks and do less or none of the unimportant tasks.

However, determining which tasks are important and which are urgent can be challenging. For a few people, this ability may come naturally, but for the vast majority, it is a skill that needs to be learned and practised. We often see two types of people: Under the same job conditions and work pressure, some are overwhelmed with paperwork, working late every day but never seeming to finish their routine tasks; others appear to handle everything effortlessly. The key difference, beyond individual work capabilities, lies in their time management methods. Despite making extensive preparations like creating numerous lists of things that need to be done and covering their desks with them, the first type fails to distinguish between urgent and important tasks or does not properly categorize tasks into quadrants. It leads to poor allocation of time resources, resulting in them being constantly busy yet disorganized.

Therefore, an important skill that managers need to learn and develop is improving their accuracy in judging the urgency and importance of tasks.

In the practical application of time management, it is crucial to learn how to distinguish whether a task is 'truly important' or 'seemingly important' and whether it is 'truly urgent' or 'seemingly urgent.'

Determining whether a task is important is crucial. The primary factor in this judgement is the task's relevance to achieving your goals, whether they are short-term or long-term. Tasks that contribute to your goals are important. On the other hand, assessing whether a task is urgent is relatively more challenging. People tend to perceive many tasks as urgent, but truly urgent tasks are not that common. Often, if you leave a task for a while, you may realize that it wasn't as urgent as it initially seemed.

Assessing the importance and urgency of tasks can be done through prior analysis as well as reverse thinking. This approach is applicable to both individuals and teams. For example, when a team faces significant difficulties or very challenging issues, they can use the 'list everything' method to list all tasks, which may initially seem important. At this point, you can allow things to continue developing and then analyse them further. Observe which tasks can be deferred or identify tasks that have a very low impact as they progress. These tasks can then be considered for removal or temporary suspension.

Many people install time-tracking apps on their phones to clearly understand where they spend a significant amount of time, such as on video apps. Uninstalling such apps can free up this time. Similarly, for teams advancing projects, if uncertainties arise, they can list tasks and move forward. Upon review, tasks that consume much effort without yielding benefits can be eliminated. By gradually removing these tasks, the team can focus more on the most important priorities. Once tasks are accurately categorized into quadrants, time can be systematically planned and allocated to accomplish them.

When using the time management Four Quadrants, another challenge lies in how to handle 'important and urgent tasks' versus 'important but not urgent tasks.'

Most people are often busy dealing with important and urgent matters. During time management training sessions I conducted within the company, I surveyed participants and found that 90% of them often had their work plans interrupted by unexpected tasks. When faced with tasks that are both important and urgent, neglecting them could lead to significant consequences, so they are temporarily prioritized over other tasks. At the end of each day, many feel like firefighters, constantly putting out fires.

It's understandable to address important and urgent tasks immediately, but one question remains worth pondering: What does consistently handling these tasks mean? What consequences does it bring about?

Most managers in companies are least willing to handle a sudden report from a subordinate about an important matter they've never heard of before, requiring an immediate decision. This reluctance stems from the fact that anyone, even if highly capable, faces a high risk of failure when dealing with something new without any prior preparation. Even if they manage to succeed once by chance, mistakes are bound to happen sooner or later. Constantly dealing with important and urgent matters is akin to an athlete continuously training their core muscles without rest, which can lead to muscle strain. Moreover, during busy times, people tend to become irritable and prone to anxiety. When the mindset is compromised, it further increases the likelihood of making mistakes.

Urgency implies a reduction in thinking time. Before fully understanding and clarifying the whole matter, rushing to make judgements and decisions greatly increases the likelihood of errors in judgement and decision-making.

On the contrary, for something important, if you can allocate sufficient time beforehand to think through and understand it thoroughly, even discussing it with relevant individuals to gather adequate information, there is a greater likelihood of success when making decisions and taking action.

Therefore, the essence of time management lies, on the one hand, in following the Pareto Principle, focusing time on the crucial 20% of tasks. On the other hand, it involves minimizing important and urgent matters by handling important tasks when they are not urgent.

Multiple waves of the COVID-19 pandemic posed significant challenges to the management of operations at Digital China. The finance, middle platform and human resources departments served as the central management safeguards, ensuring the company's basic operations were unaffected by the pandemic while safeguarding the personal and mental health of employees and complying with national control measures.

To address the uncertain risks brought by the pandemic, the company developed several contingency plans in advance. These plans preemptively deployed responses to potential emergency issues arising from the pandemic, thereby transforming potential important and urgent matters into important but not urgent tasks.

For the sake of normal workflow, every employee was encouraged to bring their laptops daily to prepare for potential temporary lockdowns, and online meetings were promoted for collaboration. To safeguard logistics, daily summaries of the shipping and receiving conditions at various warehouses were compiled, and contingency plans were formulated for situations where normal warehousing operations were disrupted and regular disinfection is conducted. To ensure normal financial and contract processes, multiple backups of commonly used seals, financial seals, bidding seals and business license certificates were made across different locations. Electronic signatures were encouraged, finance and legal personnel carry key UKEY devices, and significant payments were arranged in advance.

Of course, in the implementation of specific policies, each department considered its business positioning and carefully evaluated the policy structure. Temporary policies were adjusted promptly based on external economic conditions, avoiding one-size-fits-all approaches. Through such coordinated planning in advance, the company was able to maintain normal operations amid the challenges posed by the pandemic.

So, how can we place work as much as possible into the 'important but not urgent' quadrant? The core of this question lies in planning for important matters and ensuring that this plan serves strategic objectives. Whether for businesses or individuals, it's crucial to control desires and focus on personal goals during growth. Planning guides us in accomplishing many tasks proactively in this process.

A common issue may occur when we plan: Plans may not keep up with changes. In such cases, it's essential to learn to build flexibility into plans, which is a principle to consider in time management. Allowing for flexibility ensures that there is enough time to think during critical moments.

COORDINATE TIME WITH A SCHEDULE

After completing the quadrant analysis and determining the importance and urgency of tasks, the next step is to schedule tasks of different categories into the calendar.

Through the process of filling out the schedule, we can more accurately distinguish, arrange and verify tasks. We decide when to schedule tasks, identifying what is important and urgent and requiring immediate attention. Through continuous iteration, the schedule becomes clearer and more directive over time.

Many accomplished individuals maintain the habit of keeping a schedule. Benjamin Franklin was not only a renowned scientist and politician in the United States but also a publisher, printer, journalist, writer, philanthropist, diplomat and inventor. A crucial leader during the American Revolutionary War, he was involved in drafting several important documents. Franklin also served as the US Ambassador to France, successfully persuading France to support American independence.

His ability to achieve so much was not only due to his abundant energy but also to his disciplined approach to time management. Franklin meticulously organized his daily routines into a schedule, specifying when he would work and when he would rest, which contributed significantly to his accomplishments.

Here is an excerpt of his daily schedule:

5 am to 7 am: Wake up, wash, pray. Plan the day unfolding ahead. Read and study. Have breakfast. During this time, he would pose a meaningful question to himself: "What meaningful things will I do today?"

8 am to 11 am: Work diligently, executing the day's plan effectively.

12 pm to 1 pm: Read or review accounts. Have lunch.

2 pm to 5 pm: Work on pending tasks promptly, carefully review completed work, and promptly correct any errors.

6 pm to 9 pm: Organize belongings and return items to their places. Dinner, music, entertainment or conversation. Reflect on the day: "What meaningful things did I accomplish today?"

9 pm to 4 am: Sleep.

A detailed schedule also serves another purpose: to review the flow and use of time. When completing a task, reviewing the schedule can reveal where time has been spent and identify past time management mistakes. It helps recognize which tasks consumed unnecessary time, prompting consideration of whether to revise plans or adjust goals accordingly.

Regarding the use of schedules, a participant's experience from the DCITS Time Management Training Course is highly insightful and worth borrowing ideas from.

In my first ten years at the company, my approach to time management was more of a bottom-up process. Specifically, I handled numerous tasks one by one until I felt satisfied with their completion. I believed that by completing each task well, the overall outcome would naturally be satisfactory. However, as time went on, I realized that time management shouldn't just be about accumulating task after task. It requires a panoramic view of time management strategies.

With this panoramic view of time management, you can plan how to allocate your time for the year ahead. Determine how much time to dedicate to daily tasks, how much to focus on driving key initiatives, how much to spend on team communication and development, and how much to allocate for personal learning. By adopting a top-down approach like this, you can establish a framework for effective time management.

In this top-down approach, what does 'top' mean? I believe it's the goal. What are the most important job responsibilities in management positions? Our financial system requires understanding and breaking down the three words 'capital, funds, assets.' How can we comprehensively encompass important matters within these three words? Then, based on this foundation, construct a panoramic view of time management.

So, first, you need to determine your work objectives, then break them down, and design how much time and energy to allocate to each item. A crucial step here is to confirm with your superiors. Are your thoughts correct? Is this what your leaders think? If your work objectives haven't been confirmed with your leadership, there's a high chance you could be spending a lot of effort on tasks that don't align with company goals. Alternatively, you might be investing significant energy in daily tasks without advancing key initiatives.

After confirming the objectives, the next step is to schedule important tasks into your calendar and prioritize allocating time for them. Only by scheduling these tasks and blocking out specific time slots can you ensure that unexpected events do not disrupt your progress. Even if unforeseen events occur, scheduling allows for proper rearrangement to ensure that your planned activities can still be carried out effectively.

Take me for example. After taking on the CFO role at DCITS, I worked out a two-month time plan for myself. This plan was divided into six specific aspects.

1. Communication with the financial system personnel, including understanding the specific backgrounds of relevant individuals through human resources and conducting one-on-one interviews with core team members.
2. Foundational financial information of the company, including major financial process systems, legal entity structure, financial accounting system, expense management system, tax risk assessment reports, capital needs assessment, bank credit limits, company signing authorities and investment company status.
3. Determining important special topics based on the first two items, such as disposal plans for major risk issues.
4. Budgeting and performance tracking management.
5. External relationship handover, including audit, credit banks, tax authorities and regulatory bodies.
6. Board of directors' procedures.

The total planned time was eight weeks, and to allow for flexibility, I broke down each listed item into a six-week plan. At the end of each week, I marked completed tasks in green, delayed tasks in yellow and important reminders in red. This visual representation provided a clear overview of which tasks were completed on schedule and which ones were delayed, and it identified potential issues. For instance, tasks with significant risks identified would be prioritized for follow-up after the transition period, becoming key management focuses.

Management guru Peter Drucker also advocates for this method. In his book, *The Effective Executive*, Drucker mentions that "The first step toward executive effectiveness is therefore to record actual time use." According to Drucker, effective managers are adept at time recording and regularly review these records monthly. Through these reviews, they often discover instances where they have wasted time on trivial matters. This practice is a form of management exercise; only through repeated practice can one learn to manage time effectively and avoid deviations in time usage. Therefore, a schedule based on the Eisenhower Matrix can solve many problems.

Of course, many people encounter difficulties when filling out their schedules, such as struggling to determine the position of each task in the quadrants. There's no one-size-fits-all solution to this problem. Accuracy in scheduling requires experience and a deep understanding of the work, clearly knowing the essence and purpose of each task. Only then can one effectively fill out the schedule and prioritize tasks accordingly.

MAKE EFFECTIVE USE OF WEEKLY WORK REPORTS

Every Sunday afternoon or evening, employees of Digital China, from the CEO to grassroots staff, all independently engage in the same activity: writing weekly work reports. Utilizing their free time over the weekend, everyone takes a moment to summarize the completion status of key tasks for the week, organize the main tasks for the upcoming week, and plan and arrange work for the following week. This seemingly simple standard practice has been consistently upheld by hundreds of middle and senior managers in the company for over five years.

The weekly report system at Digital China started in 2017. At that time, I noticed issues within the group, such as a slow work pace, scattered efforts and a lack of planning – warning signs that needed to be addressed early to avoid serious consequences. To resolve these issues, I introduced the practice of weekly work reports within the company. A standardized weekly report template was designed, including a summary of the week's work and plans for the next week. It required department heads and above to fill out the reports and send them to relevant parties via email. However, the content requirements at that time were relatively simple; managers were only asked to 'list everything' by summarizing key tasks, unexpected events, and routine work in a format that listed everything.

Many people view the tool of a weekly work report as much like the concept of time management – it's considered fundamental, but in practice, it can be overused. Some individuals engage in 'showcasing' by filling out reports in a superficial way, while some supervisors only enforce formal requirements without providing substantive feedback. These practices have turned the weekly work report into a formalistic task in the management process, failing to truly assist employees in advancing their work. These various issues have tarnished the reputation of the weekly work report in workplaces, leading to resistance and scepticism among employees.

Given the prevailing circumstances, our company was no exception. Therefore, when we initially implemented this task, even though we started by promoting it among senior executives, there was a considerable lack of understanding and plenty of open criticism and private complaints. However, I deeply understood that this tool is an effective means to stimulate organizational thinking and behavioral innovation. So, despite facing significant pressure, I persisted with this requirement.

In 2018, I expanded the methodology of time management on a larger scale by instituting changes to the weekly report system. The requirements were made more explicit, focusing the content on strategic initiatives and key tasks, thereby increasing alignment. Concurrently, management training sessions were conducted. The weekly report template was enhanced from its original form to include quarterly work plans, which detailed task breakdowns and monthly objectives. Quarterly updates were incorporated into the weekly reports for comparative analysis. Descriptions of key tasks were supplemented with sections on 'issues encountered and solutions' and 'matters requiring company decision' to expedite management decision-making processes.

In 2019, building upon the template from the previous year, we continued to expand the usage of the weekly report system. The weekly report became a tool used conscientiously by the management team for self-management. The human resources department organized and established dimensions and standards for evaluating the weekly reports, conducting regular inspections and implementing a feedback mechanism to encourage improvements. We intensified efforts in communication, promotion and inspections. As a result, there was a noticeable improvement in personal planning and focus on key tasks among individuals, as well as a significant enhancement in strategic and consensus building among management teams at all levels.

In 2020, we began promoting the use of an online weekly reporting system across all staff, strengthening the planned, consistent and phased outcomes of time management at all levels through digital management. Specifically, this involved breaking down strategic key tasks, refining broad work content, and ensuring responsibilities, goal decomposition and milestone settings within each team, thereby improving the execution of strategic key tasks. Simultaneously, we established a system for inspecting, reporting and penalizing weekly reports, where each management team reviewed and provided feedback on report submissions, aiming for continuous improvement. Through this year's practices, the management team significantly strengthened their awareness of task decomposition and planning, unified the management language across all levels, and notably increased effective time investment in key tasks among team members.

In 2021, starting from strategic advancement and team building, I continuously upgraded and iterated the weekly reporting system. Guided by task objectives and using the weekly report as a focal point, emphasis was placed on the four elements of management: planning, organizing, coordinating and controlling. This effort aimed to enhance the team's execution capability further and was specifically implemented in the following four aspects.

First, there should be consistency in strategic objectives. Breaking down strategic goals and determining the responsibilities and tasks of each team member one by one ensures consensus in their understanding of responsibilities and key tasks. The hierarchical decomposition of task objectives achieves consistency between annual tasks, quarterly breakdowns and weekly plans.

Second, primary tasks should be sufficiently focused. The headers of the weekly report system prominently display annual primary tasks to remind everyone to focus their time on these tasks through frequent visibility. Additionally, the backend management system of the weekly reports conducts statistical analysis on each key task, showing the progress of numerical tasks completed.

Third, task progress should be continuously tracked. Emphasize the spirit of resolution like 'leaving a mark on the iron tool we clutch,' filling in the progress of key tasks weekly to demonstrate the entire process of implementing plans, thereby achieving the actual implementation of key work.

Fourth, the weekly report inspection management system should be implemented. Assess the submission rate of weekly reports, evaluate the effectiveness of time management by quarterly assessment for management teams and provide timely feedback on evaluation results.

Over the past five years, from initially filling out weekly reports passively to now using them consciously, they have become the fundamental tools for self-time management and team time management for all levels of the company, gaining increasing recognition from more and more people.

Under the influence of the weekly routine, everyone has gradually discovered the many benefits brought by the weekly reports. Whether in team collaboration or personal work planning, it serves as a serious yet gentle partner, earnestly urging each person in our organization to grow continuously.

At the same time, everyone recognizes that writing weekly work reports is not merely a detailed 'running account' of tasks, nor is it simply drawing up a 'schedule.' Rather, it involves summarizing and reflecting on key tasks on a weekly basis: Did the work for the week proceed as planned? What issues were encountered, and what solutions were implemented? What suggestions do we have for the company? What kind of resource support and decision-making advice do we need from superiors? What are the plans for the next week? What are the output goals? Superiors review these reports promptly and provide feedback accordingly.

Work reports from different positions and levels, though their contents vary, all focus on one theme: What is the relationship between my work and the company's strategic upgrade and performance growth? How does my work contribute value creation to the company's strategy and performance? The company has decomposed its strategies and goals into the key tasks of each critical position, breaking them down into each quarter, each month and even each week.

Of course, during the implementation of work reports, we have also undergone cognitive evolution on how to utilize this tool better and have updated the work report system several times.

In 2018, version 1.0 focused on annual key tasks while also considering daily work. In 2019, version 2.0 established a connection between key tasks and weekly work arrangements. In 2020, version 3.0

eliminated daily work reporting, placing greater emphasis on key tasks and requiring estimation of the allocation proportion for key tasks. In 2021, version 4.0 introduced the confirmation of job responsibilities and encouraged weekly summaries and communication.

The entire revision process followed several main threads. First, there was an increasing **focus on key tasks**. Second, there was a clearer **definition of job responsibilities and outputs**, increasingly guided by goals. Third, there was a growing **emphasis on reflection and communication**. At the same time, the writing and response rate of work reports became a focal point in our organizational management. This is because work reports are not merely tools for subordinates to report to superiors but also tools for organizing thoughts and facilitating networked written communication within the organization. Through writing weekly reports, individuals can better assess their work. By sharing reports, subordinates can understand the focus of their superiors, superiors can grasp the dynamics of their subordinates' work and peer collaborators can understand each other's work arrangements and thoughts. Through mutual feedback via reports, internal communication and collaboration within the organization can become smoother.

When writing work reports becomes a good work habit, both individuals and organizations benefit greatly. Writing weekly work reports integrates core time management tools such as listing everything, using the quadrant method, focusing on key tasks and summarizing work. Doing so compels us to focus our work on the most important tasks continuously. If all members of an organization can integrate time management into their daily work in this way, the combat effectiveness of the entire team can undergo a qualitative leap.

DELEGATION MEANS MANAGING LESS BUT BETTER

When mentioning Zhuge Liang, the wise strategist of the Three Kingdoms period, people often recall his famous saying: "I'll exert my utmost to fulfil my duties until death." Zhuge Liang, with his outstanding talent and dedicated spirit, assisted Liu Bei in achieving remarkable accomplishments and establishing the dominance of Shu Han. However, his consistent hands-on approach not only left him exhausted but also prevented his subordinates from fully displaying their abilities. In the end, none of his subordinates could succeed him, leading to the lamentable situation in the Shu State, where only a mediocre commander, Liao Hua, led the army due to the shortage of great generals, creating a helpless situation where 'when the tiger is absent, a monkey becomes king.'

In fact, the most appropriate time management tool for Zhuge Liang would have been delegation. If he had learned to delegate effectively, giving his subordinates more opportunities to develop and grow faster, perhaps there wouldn't have been the lament, "He died before achieving victory, causing heroes after him to weep bitterly."

In the workplace, we often observe managers adopting vastly different approaches to their work.

Some managers meticulously analyse their work, assessing feasibility, potential challenges and current resources. They develop work plans and allocate specific tasks to each subordinate. They prepare all the work themselves and actively participate in the entire process, from problem-solving to closely monitoring progress until the project is completed. If issues arise, they collaborate with their employees to find solutions.

Some managers decentralize the authority to plan specific tasks, entrusting their subordinates to think through and decide how to complete the work. They refrain from telling their subordinates "how to do it." When issues arise, these managers rarely act as 'firefighters'; instead, they expect their subordinates to find solutions independently.

The former type of manager plays the role of a 'nanny,' taking responsibility for everything, which leads to great exhaustion for themselves. Subordinates become overly reliant on them, losing their independence. Even for minor issues, subordinates habitually seek their help, resulting in low efficiency not only for the manager but also for the entire team. In contrast, the latter type of manager achieves true delegation by sharing power with subordinates, granting them full decision-making authority. This approach not only boosts their motivation but also nurtures them into capable individuals who can take on responsibilities independently.

Therefore, effective delegation is a time management skill that every manager must possess.

Delegation is actually quite simple: It involves granting the appropriate authority to others to achieve their goals. It allows them to analyse resources and conditions, anticipate potential problems, find solutions and develop work plans. By doing so, they are given the necessary authority and capability to complete their tasks effectively.

Specifically, effective delegation can be achieved through four steps:

STEP 1: UNDERSTAND AND ASSESS THE POTENTIAL RISKS OF DELEGATION

Delegation is a 'double-edged sword.' On the one hand, it can bring significant benefits to the company, such as increasing work efficiency, stimulating employee creativity and initiative, and freeing managers from trivial tasks. On the other hand, it can also bring some potential risks. Generally speaking, delegation represents an increase in responsibility and a reduction in supervision. If the capabilities and sense of responsibility of the delegate do not match the responsibilities they undertake, and if there is a lack of proper supervision during the execution process, some risks may arise. For example, delegation gives subordinates greater authority over personnel and business matters, allowing them to handle work and solve problems more quickly and independently, thereby improving the overall efficiency of the company and contributing to the achievement of corporate goals. It appears to be a win-win for both employees and the company. However, we must be clear about one thing: All of this is based on the premise that the delegate can properly use the authority, is capable of taking on the assigned responsibilities, and performs at an adequate level!

But what if the delegate does not possess such capabilities?

The general manager of a home appliance company devised a delegation plan to simplify processes, reduce costs and increase the company's sales, giving regional managers full authority so that they could independently handle certain customer requests without going through multiple levels of approval from higher-ups. This plan includes making minor price adjustments to existing products, transferring goods from other regions and adding additional services.

Although the general manager's intention was good, some issues arose during the execution process. Some regional managers set prices very low and even added extra services without principles in an effort to attract more customers. One regional manager even sold products worth about 500,000 RMB on credit to a customer who had not yet paid a deposit. Another regional manager reduced the product price by 10% to receive kickbacks.

These situations led to a significant decrease in profit margins, despite the fact that new products sold very well in the market and customer satisfaction remained high.

The scenario in this case is not uncommon. It is evident that if the capabilities of the delegate do not match the responsibilities, it can lead to unnecessary losses for the company. Therefore, before delegating, managers should first understand the potential risks of delegation and conduct an initial risk assessment. If the risk exceeds the company's tolerance, they should promptly halt the delegation or adjust the methods and approaches of delegation.

STEP 2: IMPROVE CORPORATE SYSTEMS AND IMPLEMENT STANDARDIZED MANAGEMENT

To prevent the company from falling into the 'trap' of delegation, before delegating, managers must ensure that the company's operational management has established comprehensive and supporting systems and achieved standardization. Only on this basis can the responsibilities, powers and interests of various business departments and positions be clearly defined, reducing the arbitrariness and blind spots in delegation, thereby making delegation systematic and rule-based.

By improving corporate systems, the delegator can have a clearer understanding of their own powers and responsibilities, identifying what can be delegated and what cannot, effectively avoiding overstepping or improper delegation. The delegate can clearly understand the boundaries and scope of their authorization and responsibilities, fully utilizing their power within possible limits to achieve set goals in the best possible way.

With the assurance of systems and standards, delegation can be placed under effective corporate supervision, increasing the transparency of delegation and making the rights and obligations of both the delegator and delegate clearer. This practice provides the foundation for smooth delegation management.

STEP 3: EVALUATE SUBORDINATES TO DETERMINE THEIR SUITABILITY FOR DELEGATION

Once the feasibility of delegation is established, the next step for managers is to evaluate subordinates to determine if they meet the conditions for delegation.

Generally, the higher the competence of the delegate, the greater the likelihood of successful delegation and the lower the risk. Some managers unquestioningly delegate tasks to employees who are not capable, resulting in poor work outcomes and negative impacts on the company. Therefore, before delegating, managers should rigorously assess the competence of the delegate.

For example, a technical director at Digital China once appointed a newly hired employee from Generation Y to lead an important R&D project. The employee felt very anxious because he had never been entrusted with such a significant task and had no experience handling large projects independently. The technical director reassured him, saying, "Since I dare to delegate to you, it means I fully trust your abilities. Just go ahead and do it confidently; I believe you will do well."

The technical director's confidence was not baseless. Before delegating, he conducted an investigation into the employee's character, professional skills and work attitude, which allowed him to delegate confidently.

His judgement was correct. The employee accepted the task, worked diligently and was willing to explore new solutions. Not only did he complete the R&D project, but he also successfully handled several other important projects in the following years.

The evaluation of the delegate's suitability focuses on three main aspects. First, assess whether they possess the skills and qualities corresponding to their responsibilities, such as the professional knowledge, work experience and competency level needed to complete the work, the focus, judgement and decision-making abilities required to achieve goals, and the ability to manage and integrate resources. Second, evaluate whether they have the confidence to take on responsibilities. An employee who is confident, willing to accept challenges proactively and finds ways to overcome difficulties is likely to be better prepared, more dedicated and more ambitious than one who passively accepts tasks. Third, assess whether they have good character and professional ethics, including their ability to see the big picture, adherence to company policies and teamwork spirit.

The evaluation results of the delegate's suitability not only help managers determine whether the person is worthy of delegation and what level of delegation is appropriate but also assist in identifying the company's core talent and key personnel for development.

STEP 4: GRADUALLY IMPLEMENT THE DELEGATION PLAN

Nothing is accomplished overnight, and delegation is no exception. Developing a reasonable delegation plan and gradually implementing it is necessary to make the delegation truly effective.

It is important to note that a prerequisite for delegation is that it must be based on trust.

Many managers make the mistake of simultaneously delegating and doubting their subordinates, leading to ineffective power transitions and making subordinates feel uncomfortable due to the lack of trust, reducing their work efficiency and lowering the company's performance. Ultimately, the delegation becomes merely a formality.

Renowned management guru Stephen Covey once said, "Trust and delegation are the pathways to effective delegation." Once you delegate, you must give employees sufficient trust, allowing them to view the company as a platform where they can fully realize their ambitions. In practice, employees hope to gain their superior's trust and be granted more authority. At the same time, employees who are trusted completely can make autonomous decisions and effectively exercise the powers they have been given.

Trust not only stems from the manager's full confidence in the employees but also arises from a positive atmosphere of mutual trust. Only with mutual trust can delegation continue sustainably. Delegation, coupled with trust, can motivate employees to perform their duties well and even significantly exceed the expectations of the delegated tasks.

Kōnosuke Matsushita showed great trust in his subordinates when delegating tasks. In 1926, he planned to open a new office in Kanazawa, Japan. He approached a young employee, only 19 years old, and said to him, "I intend to open an office in Kanazawa, and I believe you are the right person for the job. Go to Kanazawa, find a suitable location and rent an office space. Let me know how much funding you need, and I will provide you with full support."

The young man was very surprised because he couldn't believe that the boss would entrust him with such an important task. After arriving in Kanazawa, he immediately began his work, writing daily letters to Matsushita to report his progress. Matsushita replied, "You don't need to report to me every day. A quarterly report is sufficient. I have complete confidence in your abilities, so go ahead and do your best."

The young man was deeply moved, and eventually, the Kanazawa office thrived, generating substantial profits for the Matsushita Group.

Such examples are commonplace in the Panasonic Corporation. For instance, the company never keeps trade secrets from its employees. On the first day of work, new employees receive comprehensive technical training without any reservations. Some people worry about this approach, fearing that it might lead to the company's trade secrets being leaked. However, Matsushita said, "When you hire these employees into your company, you must fully trust them. If you withhold technical information to protect trade secrets, employees will lack familiarity with their tasks during production. This will inevitably lead to an increase in defective products and higher costs for the company. Consequently, the company would suffer greater losses."

While summarizing his management experience, Matsushita once said that by using this trust-based delegation approach, his company had never encountered any failures. Trusting people is a very important condition for cultivating excellent employees.

Therefore, trust is the foundation of delegation, and delegation must be based on full trust in employees. Once you delegate, you should have no reservations and give subordinates sufficient space to allow them opportunities to perform. Doing so will enable them to fully showcase their talents on the company platform and achieve a great sense of accomplishment, ultimately benefiting the company.

Of course, trust does not mean that managers can ignore everything from then on. During the delegation process, timely monitoring and tracking are also essential. Delegation is not about letting go entirely; proper delegation should be relative, principled and under effective supervision.

To achieve effective delegation, it is also necessary to establish an effective supervision and inspection mechanism. Inspection is a process that has nothing to do with trust or distrust. Without this process, delegating would be built on a blind and disorganized foundation, and 'delegating power' would be equivalent to 'abandoning power,' leading to various problems and potentially catastrophic consequences for the company.

Delegation is like flying a kite: You need to be brave enough to let go yet still hold onto the string to prevent the kite from losing control. If you only hold without letting go, the kite will never fly. Conversely, if you only let go without holding, the kite will either fail to lift off or will lose control once in the air and eventually crash. Only by simultaneously letting go and reining in, applying appropriate control, can the kite fly high and steadily. Additionally, the kite string needs to be strong enough so that you can reel the kite back in at any time; otherwise, you risk either losing the kite or being unable to let it fly again after reeling it back. Similarly, in the process of delegation, managers must grasp this 'kite string,' which represents adequate control. Delegation should not exceed the manager's capacity to control and should be combined with reasonable supervision.

REVIEW EFFECTIVELY TO ENSURE CONTINUOUS IMPROVEMENT

In time management, summarization and review are very effective tools. However, many people do not use these tools effectively. I often see some people simply making a list of all the things that happened during a certain period when summarizing. Admittedly, this task is necessary, but it is far from being the entirety of summarization. Summarization involves a comprehensive, systematic overall inspection, evaluation, analysis and study of work over some time. It aims to identify achievements, shortcomings and lessons learned. Summarization is a rational reflection on past work that can be used to guide future work.

The essence of summarization is analysis, which we often refer to as a review. This term actually originates from the game of Go, where after a game concludes, both players retrospectively analyse the entire process to examine the strengths and weaknesses of each move, including reflecting on their thought process, why they made a certain move and how they planned and anticipated subsequent moves. This term is also commonly used in stock investing, referring to a static review of the market to gain a deeper understanding of market changes. In fact, not only in games or the stock market but also in our business, management and even our lives, we also require constant review to assess situations, capitalize on advantages and avoid pitfalls. As Will Durant eloquently summarized Aristotle's philosophy in his *The Story of Philosophy*, "We are what we repeatedly do." By actively discovering, summarizing and reflecting on issues through reviews, we can continually improve, making excellence a habit.

So, how can we effectively summarize and review? I'll use an annual summary as an example to explain the process. A yearly summary involves a comprehensive, systematic review, inspection, evaluation, analysis and reflection on the past year's work. It aims to identify achievements, uncover shortcomings, summarize the underlying causes and lessons learned and provide better guidance for the coming year's work. An effective summary is the foundation and prerequisite for formulating new work plans and budget goals for the new year, as well as a guarantee for the execution and implementation of various work plans.

A comprehensive annual summary that can guide future work should include five elements:

First, review of year-start goals. Reflect on the goals set at the beginning of the year, including business targets, key work objectives and corresponding milestones.

Second, evaluate execution results. Compare the execution results with the set goals. Identify which goals were achieved and which were not.

Third, analyse reasons. Determine the key factors for success. Identify the fundamental reasons for any failures. Distinguish between objective factors and subjective factors and identify whether the issues were related to the tasks or the people involved. From a time management perspective, analyse whether the management team was able to focus efficiently and coordinate effectively to ensure the achievement of various goals.

Fourth, summarize experiences and lessons. Evaluate whether successful experiences can serve as methods and principles to guide future work. Analyse failures to understand how to improve and avoid making the same mistakes in the future.

Fifth, set goals and work plans for the next year. Based on the previous year's summary, propose goals and work plans for the next year, ensuring logical consistency and coherence between the past and the future.

Certainly, different companies have different requirements for summaries. For example, at Digital China, the human resources department requires employees to base their annual time management summary and personal report on their job responsibility statement. The summary content includes:

- Comparison with annual task goals in the job responsibility statement. Summarize the completion status of various tasks and conduct a process management summary (including how to break down plans, organize coordination and control deviations in conjunction with weekly reports).
- Analysis of personal work gains and losses in relation to time management. Analyse the allocation of time and effort for key tasks throughout the year. Additionally, analyse personal work gains and losses from both individual and team time management perspectives.
- Evaluation of key team tasks based on personal participation. Evaluate the key tasks of the team from the perspective of personal involvement and support and provide suggestions for the team's key tasks for the next year.

The summary of 'opportunity management' work by the general manager of a business group under Digital China is worth learning from.

In 2021, our approach to opportunity management was top-down, following the principle of first rigid implementation, then optimization and finally solidification.

During the first phase of promoting this work, there was some misunderstanding among the front-end business personnel. First, we had to ensure a high level of consensus and firm execution of opportunity management by the core team of the business group. To clarify the positioning, requirements and boundaries of this work, we introduced the opportunity management regulations in March. Various smaller departments also introduced additional strengthening measures based on these regulations to ensure the scale of opportunities in the first phase and to help sales personnel gradually accept and adapt to the process.

In the second phase, we optimized, simplified and rationalized the content of opportunity management through system enhancements. We developed reports and dashboards to provide data support for sales personnel and the sales management team, improving the customer experience and strengthening the integration with business management.

In the third phase, we focused on enhancing the management team's review awareness and the quality of opportunity reporting. Starting with the core team, we reviewed one opportunity daily, guiding sales personnel toward a correct understanding and application of opportunity management.

In the fourth phase, we aimed to integrate opportunity management more closely with business processes, making it a part of the workflow rather than an isolated management module. We planned to combine the existing offline project communication, project reporting mechanisms, and the feedback and interaction functions of Customer Relationship Management (CRM) to advance control actions truly. This integration was expected to enhance the quality of opportunities further.

In reviewing that year's opportunity management work, I found several positive aspects: Opportunity management had achieved consensus at various business levels, actively promoting key projects, overall control, opportunity discovery and process management. We had established an opportunity review mechanism. Core channels[13] had been driven to transform toward a customer-centric approach and actively promote horizontal composite sales. This development led to multiple significant cross-channel cooperation projects worth tens of millions and cultivated a group of channel managers who share a common vision, goals and action plans.

However, there were still areas for improvement: The integration of opportunities with business needed to be further strengthened. While the overall framework for opportunity data and analysis was emerging, it lacked specificity. There was a need to enhance support for opportunity classification according to different business models and units to be more closely aligned with the business essence. Doing so enabled opportunity data analysis and sales behavior data analysis to support better business decision-making and daily management.

It is worth mentioning that there are three key points we need to pay particular attention to when summarizing.

KEY POINT ONE: LIST KEY TASKS BUT AVOID COVERING EVERYTHING

Summarizing key tasks involves the philosophical idea of focusing on primary contradictions. The most important lesson I learned from studying philosophy is that in all practical work, one must first address the primary contradiction, which means focusing on the key, central tasks. The key tasks in work are the 'primary issues,' and they also follow the 80/20 rule: summarize the 20% of key tasks that require 80% of your effort. Summarization is a very important learning process, and only by learning to summarize can we continuously improve and enhance our work.

When summarizing, it is especially important to note that trying to 'say everything' often results in 'saying nothing.' Therefore, please focus on the most important things and explain them clearly in the shortest time possible. Meetings, as important occasions for summarizing work, often become black holes for time wastage in enterprises. It is very common for speakers to be habitually verbose and for meeting hosts to fail to control the session, leading to extended meeting times.

If we convert income to unit working time, we can calculate a person's time cost. For example, for an ordinary employee with an annual income of 200,000 RMB, a mid-level manager with a yearly income of 500,000 RMB and a senior executive with an annual income of 1,000,000 RMB, the time cost per minute is approximately 1.6 RMB, 4 RMB and 8 RMB, respectively. Thus, an ordinary meeting involving one senior executive, three mid-level managers and two junior employees that exceeds 45 minutes would cost over 1,000 RMB. In stark contrast, consider how much sales effort and cost are required to achieve a net profit of 1,000 RMB!

Everyone can reflect on the number of meetings they usually attend and estimate how much time is wasted, which gives an idea of the extent of time wastage. Often, this is due to ineffective summarization. Good summarization is concise and to the point, with a clear focus, logical structure, rigorously filtered information, and a simple and elegant presentation style. If we fail to achieve these in our summaries, we are wasting everyone's time.

For summarization and presentation, you can refer to the PREP Framework (see Figure 3-3).

FIGURE 3-3
PREP FRAMEWORK FOR A SUMMARY STATEMENT

Of course, there are many similar methodologies, and different people have different styles of expression. It is not necessary to adopt a one-size-fits-all template for summarization. However, always remember to highlight the key points in your summary and avoid trying to cover everything.

KEY POINT TWO: EVALUATE BOTH RESULTS AND PROCESSES

Previously, we clearly listed key items through listing everything. How should we analyse and summarize the top three identified important tasks? The first step must be to focus on the results. We need to evaluate how the results are – are they good or bad, acceptable or not? That depends on our consensus on the evaluation standards. Therefore, during the planning stage, defining and describing the goals is crucial, and we must have a very clear understanding of the objectives.

Second, we need to summarize not only the outcomes but also the processes: Why did we do well? Why did we not do well enough? Why did we fail? Analysing the processes can help us identify problems and discover the underlying logic.

Western classical philosophy delves deeply into the contemplation of processes. There is a Greek myth about "Achilles and the Tortoise." Achilles, a renowned swift-footed hero in Greek mythology, is the fastest runner. However, the Greek philosopher and mathematician Zeno of Elea argued that he could never catch up to a crawling tortoise. Zeno's paradox assumes that the turtle starts 10 metres ahead of Achilles. In order for Achilles to catch up with the turtle, he must first cover those 10 metres. However, during this time, the turtle has moved forward a certain distance, and Achilles must spend more time covering this new gap. This process repeats infinitely, and Achilles can never complete the distance between him and the turtle. Once the turtle is ahead, it remains ahead forever.[14]

Indeed, this is a classic paradoxical story, but it prompts initial thoughts on the concept of 'limits.' The problem was ultimately resolved when Newton and Leibniz invented calculus. It must be noted that it was this detailed investigation into the 'process' of physical phenomena that led to the development of modern science in the West. Without studying the process, we might never understand the intrinsic logical relationships of events.

In the face of a rapidly changing global market, an enterprise's ability to respond quickly has become a key factor affecting its long-term competitiveness. Achieving this goal depends mainly on the refined control of operational processes and the analysis, mining and decision support of related process data. The process is the specific execution phase of tasks and includes a lot of detailed information. We often say, "A small ant-hole can collapse a great dyke; details determine success or failure." The crux of the problem usually lies in the details, and summarization can facilitate the review of process details.

Knowing employees doesn't come from constantly having meetings with management cadres and listening to their 'military orders' or looking at their road maps. Instead, it involves frequently visiting project teams and observing the expressions in the eyes of the team members. This way, managers can gauge the progress of the project and the fighting spirit of the project team. When we talk about enterprise practice, we must not only start from problems but also ensure its operability and emphasize the workflow of doing things. The process will reveal more detailed information.

Whether focused on goals or processes, the key to effective summarization lies in the thought methodology and the basic principles for judging right and wrong. The nature of things does not change because of our summaries; rather, through summarization, our ability and level of understanding are enhanced. It allows us to make fewer mistakes or avoid them altogether when we encounter similar issues in the future. The importance of summarization is reflected in this. The process of summarization helps the team develop a shared understanding and memory of the processes, making it a collective learning experience.

KEY POINT THREE: CONSIDER WHETHER YOUR WORK ALIGNS WITH THE COMPANY'S STRATEGIC GOALS

"Concentrate efforts in one direction and ensure benefits flow through one channel."[15] Everyone's efforts should converge on a single point, and everyone's benefits should be shared at that same point. Only then will the team have true execution power.

When everyone lists everything and summarizes, they should understand the key tasks at the higher level and the overall company strategy. Otherwise, no matter how much effort they put in, if it doesn't align with the key tasks of the higher level, it will be wasted effort, even if they are extremely busy. Each person must clarify how their key tasks relate to the key tasks of their superiors and how they can contribute effectively. If the goals are aligned, the work will produce substantial and effective outcomes, and the team's motivation for development will be strengthened and consolidated. If the goals do not match, adjustments must be made immediately.

The company's overall strategic goals can be broken down step by step into smaller targets for employees. That task is essentially not worth doing if someone finds that their work has no relation to the company's overall strategic direction. Alternatively, it may indicate that the team leader is not competent, as they lack a comprehensive perspective. By encouraging everyone to discuss their goals, we aim to achieve consensus, share objectives and build a common vision through the summarization process.

After reviewing the key points above, you will certainly improve your summarization work. Through continuous summarization and analysis, you will gain a better understanding of the target path and the related key factors. At the same time, you will also improve your abilities and knowledge as you share your goals and build a common vision.

CHAPTER 4

SPEND TIME ON THE MOST IMPORTANT STRATEGIC MANAGEMENT

STRATEGY IS THE CORE DRIVING FORCE OF THE ENTERPRISE

We know the value of time and learn time management techniques for better allocation of precious resources to our most important and worthwhile tasks. For a company, what is the most important task? Strategy.

The term 'strategy' originates from ancient warfare and military activities. It is a concept derived from the practice of war and military operations, referring to the tactics that can be employed in war, essentially the clever plans and procedures for defeating the enemy. As early as the Spring and Autumn period (770–476 BC), Sun Tzu wrote the widely known *The Art of War* based on past war experiences. Although it was not named a strategy, its content is imbued with rich strategic thoughts. Even today, people can still draw valuable insights from it, and it is widely used and highly influential around the world.

For a company, strategic management is crucial, as it concerns the allocation of resources and development goals. It aims to achieve greater profitability and ensure long-term survival and growth. Based on a thorough and scientific analysis of the external environment and internal conditions, strategic management involves making a comprehensive plan for the company's development goals and the means to achieve them, as well as the implementation of these plans. From this perspective, strategy is the core driving force of a company.

In our approach to time management, we must focus on the most important 20% and, in terms of a company's priorities, strategic management is arguably the most crucial 1%.

Effective strategic management is inherently linked to effective time management. Throughout the entire strategic management process – from formulation to implementation and iteration – time management plays a vital role:
- In the strategic planning phase, time management helps us penetrate the fog of time, enabling us to think from a longer-term perspective and thereby secure the future.
- When selecting strategic initiatives, time management assists us in sorting and analysing all options based on their priority, allowing us to make the wisest decisions.
- When setting strategic goals, we define the phased achievements of our strategic direction along the timeline.
- During the strategic execution phase, time management aids us in more reasonably allocating time resources to various tasks, ensuring the achievement of strategic goals.
- Reconsidering uncertainties that have changed over time and adjusting predictions is strategic refreshment and iteration.

THINK ABOUT STRATEGIC PLANNING FROM A LONGER TIME DIMENSION

When engaging in strategic planning, many companies tend to focus more on the variables that impact them, often neglecting the time dimension – that is, how long they plan to achieve their strategic goals. Differences in the time dimension lead to differences in execution methods, and naturally, the results will also vary significantly.

When companies undertake strategic planning, they must focus on the future and think from a longer-term perspective: What kind of company will it become in the future? What strategies should be implemented now to achieve this goal? How can the company stand out in market competition?

Unfortunately, I often see countless companies focusing solely on immediate gains or being overwhelmed by current troubles and issues, neglecting long-term strategic planning. As a result, these companies find themselves in a passive position or losing out in market competition a few years down the line, including some that were once highly successful.

Today, China is undergoing a period of social and economic transformation, with new changes emerging constantly. To adapt to these changes, companies must also transform, making strategic planning their top priority. In this process, we need to consider not only what kind of strategic plan to formulate but also how long it will take to achieve it. Numerous cases of failed companies warn us that if we ignore the time dimension in strategic planning, focusing only on immediate gains and losses without considering long-term development, we may struggle in the future, be caught between present realities and planned futures, and ultimately fail to reach our envisioned goals.

Digital China has adopted a cloud strategy as its future strategic plan and is comprehensively developing its cloud business precisely based on this consideration.

When Digital China was founded, it not only chose its name but also set it as a mission to transform China into a digital nation.

From its inception in 2000, when the company conducted an internal survey to design the Digital China logo, the word 'infinity' emerged as the most significant concept for everyone. If converted into a dynamic image, it first brings to mind the Milky Way – a dynamic, open cloud moving in the universe. Over the past two decades, one of the most important changes in the IT field has been the emergence of cloud technology. For Digital China, with its vision of 'digital China,' the 'cloud' is both our original intention and future direction.

In 2017, based on our assumptions and judgement about the overall trend of the digital economy and to ensure better development for Digital China in the future, we clearly identified the cloud as the core of our future growth.

To make this strategic plan, we engaged in deep reflection and evaluation. We did not focus on short-term investments and returns but rather: "What will Digital China look like in five years? What kind of company does Digital China aspire to be? What actions do we need to take now to achieve this?"

Starting from this point, we observed that China is at a critical juncture of transitioning from informatization to digitalization. This digital transformation will bring profound and long-term historic opportunities and fundamental changes to the technology industry and the entire economic operation mechanism.

Driven by the digital economy, the urgency for enterprises to undergo digital transformation is very strong. Digital transformation will drive the growth of Information and Communication Technology (ICT) investment for most enterprises.

One of the most significant changes in digital transformation is that customer demand is shifting from buying the process to purchasing the result and from buying products to buying capabilities. Enterprises do not need merely standardized IT products and equipment but also direct technological empowerment of their business processes. Cloud computing is the cornerstone of digital transformation. Many digital scenarios require applications to be deployed directly in the cloud, leveraging technologies such as big data, artificial intelligence and the Internet of Things to support the digital transformation of enterprises. The market's demands on most tech companies are shifting from the ability to develop high-tech products to the ability to meet customer needs efficiently through services and technologies. At the same time, during the process of enterprise digital transformation, a plethora of digital innovation services and new technological solutions emerging in the cloud will foster a new wave of innovation in the cloud computing market. Digital transformation will also create enormous growth opportunities from the supply side.

Furthermore, digital transformation will lead to the reinvention of business models and the restructuring of the industrial chain. As the digital transformation process deepens, the business processes and value systems of enterprise customers, manufacturers and channel service providers will undergo significant changes. The value pursuit of enterprises will shift from "enhancing organizational and business efficiency based on the company's internal needs" to "strategic transformation and business innovation based on industry development." Investments will shift from "primarily asset-based investments with supplementary service investments" to "a decrease in asset-based investments and a significant increase in service investments represented by cloud services." Decision-making mechanisms will move from being "technology department-led" to "a close integration of technology and business with joint decision-making." Technology industry vendors will experience the transition from being "product providers" focused on products with supplementary services to "function providers" focused on meeting customer needs. This shift from process-oriented to result-oriented will bring about the reengineering of business models and the reshaping of the industrial chain. In this process, channel service providers will also face significant opportunities and challenges. Enterprise digital transformation strengthens the link between customers, manufacturers and channel service providers, shifting the focus of the industrial chain further toward the client end. Suppose channel service providers can offer more value-added services and customized development based on existing standardized products to meet customer needs. They can truly become core partners and enablers who closely participate in customers' digital transformation and upgrades.

Thus, Digital China's strategic plan emerged: to become China's leading digital transformation partner. By focusing on key elements of enterprise digital transformation, the company innovatively proposed the 'data cloud integration' strategy and technical framework.[16] The emphasis is on developing product and service capabilities in cloud-native, digital-native, digital-cloud integration and the Information Technology Application Innovation (ITAI) industry. This approach aims to provide ubiquitous, agile IT capabilities and integrated data-driven capabilities to customers in various industries, including fast-moving consumer goods, retail, automotive, finance, healthcare, government, education and telecom operators, all at different stages of digital transformation. By building cross-industry integrated innovative digital business scenarios and new business models, Digital China aims to help enterprise customers establish core competencies and competitive advantages for the future, thereby comprehensively promoting the digital and intelligent transformation and upgrading of society.

Of course, formulating a strategic plan is no easy task; it requires us to focus on the future while starting actions at present. Specifically, the process of strategic planning can be roughly divided into the following three steps.

1. GAIN INSIGHTS INTO THE COMPETITIVE FIELD AND MAKE ASSUMPTIONS ABOUT THE FUTURE

In natural science, hypotheses come first. Hypotheses lead to axioms, axioms lead to theorems, and theorems lead to deductions – this is the process of scientific development. Similarly, in running a business, having a hypothesis is a crucial starting point. This hypothesis is essentially a subjective understanding of the objective world. With an understanding of the objective world and the effort to identify certainties within future uncertainties, we can recognize opportunities and risks, thus making relatively accurate strategic choices.

When analysing the competitive field, we need to focus on several key factors: the macro environment, industry trends, technology, customers, users and the market. In leadership training courses, we often invite experts to explain and analyse political, economic, social and technological trends and developments in China and the world. The goal is to enable leaders at all levels to understand the broader context, form their judgement and hypotheses, and determine Digital China's competitive fields and future development strategy based on this understanding.

In different regions and at various times, the primary external influencing factors are constantly changing. Sometimes, changes in the industry are decisively influenced by policy factors. For example, in the past decade, many new brands and opportunities have emerged in the field of domestic IT brands. At other times, macroeconomic factors such as population changes can profoundly impact certain industries. Trends such as declining birth rates and an ageing population can significantly influence the direction of the education, healthcare and insurance industries. Occasionally, the discovery and diffusion speed of new technologies plays a decisive role. For instance, the widespread adoption of mobile internet transmission and switching technology led to a surge in demand for smartphones, which subsequently increased global smartphone manufacturing capacity and rapidly developed the smartphone industry, resulting in the emergence of several world-class giants in this field.

In most cases, companies cannot control the external environment. What we must strive to do is identify various factors, track their changing trends and predict the impacts these trends will bring. Will a new technology present us with new opportunities or unexpected competitors? What new product and service opportunities might arise from the combination of several new technologies? How will changes in population, economy and socio-culture influence resource aggregation? Which economic sectors will see new demands? Which sectors might experience declining demand? Where are the talent hotspots? Are our upstream suppliers' businesses growing or declining? Will changes in the profitability of key customer industries affect their purchasing power? Can the growth of emerging customer groups create a new market where revenue covers marketing costs? By answering these questions, companies can better navigate the uncertainties of the external environment and make more informed strategic decisions.

All these influencing factors and their changing trends will, to varying degrees, impact the business development and capabilities of an organization. To seize opportunities brought by changes and mitigate the effects of adverse changes, we need to continue to gather information about the external environment comprehensively and thoroughly during the phase. This approach allows us to discern significant trends from subtle indicators, providing a solid foundation of input information for strategic formulation.

Our most traditional distribution business serves as an example for industry analysis. Figure 4-1 is a simple value chain transmission diagram. At the very top are the suppliers of semiconductors and system software, followed by brand manufacturers. After production, products move to distribution and then to agency services, where integrators, value-added distributors, retailers and independent solution providers are involved. The diagram depicts a conventional structure and does not fully encapsulate the entire industry landscape. For instance, some brand manufacturers sell products directly to users.

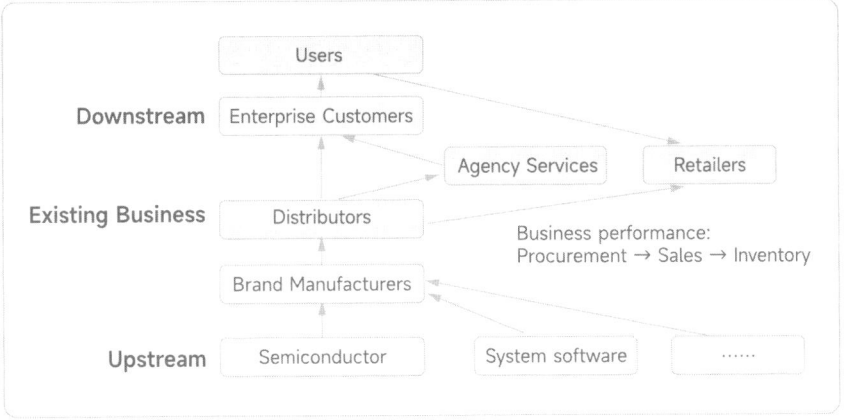

FIGURE 4-1
EXAMPLE STRUCTURE OF IT INDUSTRY ANALYSIS

It is important to note that, in many cases, the business customers and end-users are different, and we need to consider them separately. For instance, when providing solutions to a bank, the bank is the customer, but the end-users are the bank employees or the ultimate consumers. Thus, it requires us to understand the usage habits of the end-users, not just the customers' procurement process.

The entire industry's changes are complex and often driven by fundamental technological revolutions. In the IT industry, technological advancements have altered the modes of IT supply, transferring from the standalone era to the internet era and now to the cloud-native and digital-native era. IT capabilities are now being delivered as services. This service model is completed in an ecological and socialized manner. By conducting such a comprehensive industry analysis and observing the structural changes in the industry, we can identify what actions we should take.

2. LOOK INWARD – HAVE A CLEAR ASSESSMENT AND UNDERSTANDING OF YOUR COMPETITIVE ADVANTAGES

Based on our assumptions, we then examine where our competitive capabilities lie. Compared to our competitors, what advantage resources do we currently possess? What unique abilities do we have? These resources and abilities, which form our core competitive advantages, are the foundation for creating value for our customers.

Digital China's volume distribution business has a core advantage in risk-control capabilities. Large-scale product distribution requires significant capital, and if there is a lack of risk control in the repayment from the next-level sales channels, the company will face considerable financial risk. Over more than 20 years, we have established a rigorous risk-control system. For example, when evaluating the credit of our next-level channel partners, we not only assess the channel partners themselves but also delve into their end customers. By understanding who the channel partners sell to, we can evaluate the repayment risk of the channel partners. This approach allows us to adjust our risk-control level based on the end customers' credit values, resulting in a more comprehensive and reliable risk assessment system.

If the channel partners sell products to large central enterprises, the credit value in this chain is high, resulting in lower risks. Conversely, if the products are sold to small and medium-sized enterprises, the risk is higher. Additionally, the creditworthiness of some end-industry customers can be influenced by macro policies. At the early stages of an industry, substantial government subsidies may enhance purchasing power, but once overcapacity occurs and subsidies are withdrawn, payment abilities may become problematic. If we cannot extend our credit evaluation to include end customers, such risks cannot be anticipated in advance.

The comprehensive risk-control capability described above is our core competency. Therefore, when conducting strategic analysis, we should consider whether such core competencies can be transformed into services that we offer to our partners, thereby expanding the scope of our business.

―――――――

The above is a brief example of competitive advantage analysis. When formulating a strategy, it is crucial to analyse our advantages thoroughly. It is essential for progress, as the starting point for any new business is based on leveraging even the slightest advantage. Without any advantage, it would not be easy to advance the business.

3. CLARIFY KEY INITIATIVES TO TURN ADVANTAGES INTO WINNING

Once we have identified our competitive landscape and thoroughly analysed our advantages, we can pinpoint the shortcomings that need to be addressed and the strengths that can be leveraged. This clarity helps us define our key initiatives.

―――――――

For example, one of our businesses can reach many customers, but our sales only account for a small percentage of their procurement budgets. Can we take two years to improve service to our top five customers, striving to increase their procurement share with us and ultimately become their largest supplier? It could be our key initiative and a focal point for our efforts. Similarly, for new business development, we can leverage our existing strengths in particular industries by turning our current customers into a niche market for new business. Such initiatives should be derived from a thorough analysis of our strengths and weaknesses rather than mindlessly following competitors. This process of analysis and execution requires both imagination and the agility to implement quickly.

By following these steps and thinking carefully at each stage, we can develop a scientific and long-term strategic plan.

As the saying goes, "Plan for the long term." It reflects the profound wisdom handed down by our ancestors. Being far-sighted means having a broader vision and a longer time horizon. Strategic planning conducted with this vision and time frame often provides greater guidance for the company. When we tirelessly and steadfastly work towards achieving this long-term strategic plan, we naturally focus on the priorities, dedicating our time and energy to the most important tasks. Consequently, the immediate challenges and gains or losses become insignificant.

DISTINGUISH PRIORITIES AND MAKE WISE CHOICES

When selecting key measures, corporate managers often face multiple options, which can cause confusion and make it difficult to decide which one to choose. Such dilemmas are particularly common during periods of transformation, where such choices frequently arise and can be especially challenging. After all, the selection of key measures directly impacts the development of the company, and one wrong move could lead to total failure.

At this point, various time management methods come into play.

We can first use the listing everything method to enumerate the numerous strategic measures the company faces and then identify the most important 20% among them. Of course, for crucial decisions related to strategy, even 20% is too broad. In such cases, we need to use the four-quadrant method to distinguish between urgency and importance, identifying the most critical and urgent measure from this 20% of key strategic measures.

That is how DCITS's technology route system of core banking was chosen.

As the name suggests, the core banking system is the most crucial IT system in a bank, providing essential services such as customer information processing, deposit and loan products, payment services and general ledger management. DCITS's core banking system, which began in 2003, not only broke the market monopoly held by foreign vendors but also provided high-performance product support for the development of domestic banks. It allowed many small and medium-sized banks in China to afford the costs of core infrastructure, significantly enhancing the technological level of domestic banks. By 2021, the core banking system had ranked first in the domestic market for several consecutive years.[17]

However, during the Double 11 (Single's Day) shopping festival in 2013, the high concurrency of massive instant transactions made us realize that the internet would profoundly transform the banking business model. This change was not limited to mere channel expansion; the Chinese banking industry would also face this reality. Amid the overwhelming wave of the internet, an internal debate arose within Digital China: is distributed technology suitable for banking operations?

This now seemingly unquestionable issue was highly controversial at the time. The prevailing industry opinion then was that distributed technology was not suitable for core banking systems, which require very high data consistency for critical transactions. However, some technical experts within DCITS believed that the challenges brought by the internet were inevitable for the future of banking. Choosing distributed technology meant abandoning the established architecture and product systems and starting anew from scratch. Ultimately, DCITS decided to adopt distributed technology to build a new generation of core banking systems.

The decision was difficult, and the actual development process encountered even greater challenges. Choice of distributed technology required solving the issue of 'transaction consistency';[18] otherwise, implementation would be impossible. Banking business scenarios are highly complex, and unlike the internet, which allows for a certain fault tolerance, financial-grade distributed applications demand absolute precision. The difficulty levels are not on the same scale, and there was no industry experience from which to draw.

The technical team, undaunted by challenges, carefully verified and boldly experimented, finding reasonable solutions through repeated trial and error. To address the issue of transaction consistency in financial scenarios, they innovated the 'Virgo Financial Distributed Transaction Middleware'; to tackle the shortcomings of distributed data capabilities in the financial sector, they developed the 'Libra Data Distributed Middleware.' In 2015, they successfully launched the industry's first financial-grade distributed technology platform, Sm@rtGalaxy, which provided a comprehensive distributed solution tailored to banking transaction system scenarios. Based on this technology platform, they released the industry's first commercial 'distributed core banking system' in 2016, which was quickly adopted by several banks, including Zhongguancun Bank, aiBank and Bank of Fuxin.

Adopting the forward-looking design concept of 'distributed + microservices + cloud-native,' DCITS's distributed core banking system, Sm@rtEnsemble has continuously iterated, refining the entire distributed application architecture. The success of DCITS's distributed core banking system spurred domestic technology vendors to follow suit, comprehensively advancing the application of distributed technology in the banking technology sector. It allowed DCITS's financial core services to consistently move from victory to victory, maintaining its industry's dominant leading position.

For DCITS's business, the core banking system is the critical 20%; for the core system, the 'distributed' technology direction is the crucial 20%. By seizing these two key 20%, DCITS's financial technology strategy has achieved a strategic high ground of technical, product and market leadership.

It is essential to emphasize that in a constantly changing competitive environment, the choice of strategic measures requires a comprehensive analysis and assessment of the company's capabilities and the external environment. For example, we need to determine the company's existing core competencies. That is because when selecting strategic measures, a company should focus on business areas where its core competencies can be fully utilized. Additionally, factors such as the technological characteristics of the industry, its life cycle, and the company's competitive position within the industry are crucial considerations when choosing strategic measures. These factors need thorough analysis but will not be elaborated on here.

BREAK DOWN KEY MEASURES INTO WEEKLY REPORTS TO ENSURE STRATEGIC IMPLEMENTATION

After identifying key measures through time management methods, how can we ensure these measures are actually implemented? Doing so requires us to break them down step by step, from annual plans to quarterly and monthly plans, and finally down to weekly work reports (see Figure 4-2).

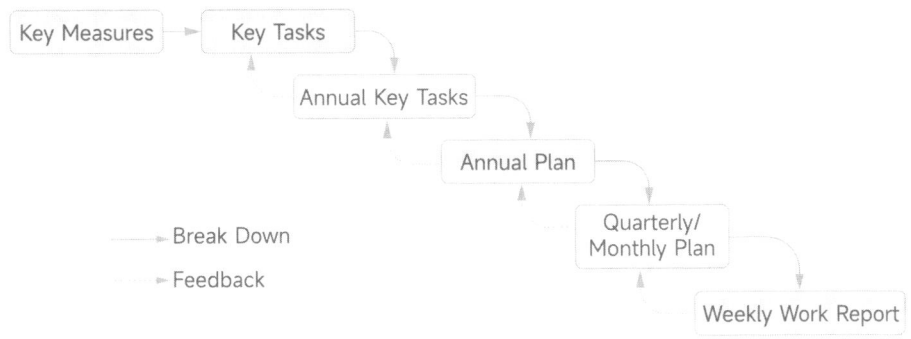

FIGURE 4-2
BREAKDOWN OF KEY TASKS

In this process, we need to apply the 80/20 rule of time management to first identify 20% of key measures among all strategic initiatives, analyse and break them down, and then find the 20% of key tasks from those measures. Following this method, we continue to break down the key tasks into annual key tasks, annual plans, quarterly plans, monthly plans and, finally, weekly work reports. Through this layered breakdown, each important measure is detailed, including what tasks need to be completed by whom each week. Strategy is no longer an elusive vision but can be translated into everyone's daily work. Whether it is a visit, a meeting or a document, all tasks are aligned with key work content and serve the company's strategy. The implementation of the strategy naturally becomes a smooth process.

That is how DCITS's marketing work for a certain industry product has achieved strategic implementation.

In more than 20 years of informatization and digitalization construction, DCITS has accumulated very deep solution capabilities, which are not only due to the company's technical strength but also closely related to the strategic breakdown and execution of the marketing team. Five years ago, during the intensive expansion of a certain industry market, the marketing team conducted a business status analysis, market analysis, customer analysis and team analysis and then formulated a three-year development strategy – the New Customer Expansion, Key Account Marketing, Strategic Project Wins, and Balanced Solution Sales (MKSB) Plan (see Table 4-1).

	First Year	Second Year	Third Year
M Plan: New Customer Expansion	At least five new customers, contract amount of 20 million RMB	At least ten new customers, contract amount of 40 million RMB	At least 15 new customers each year, contract amount of 60 million RMB
K Plan: Key Account Marketing	Secure three key accounts with contracts worth over 10 million RMB each	Secure eight key accounts with contracts worth over 10 million RMB each	Secure 15 key accounts with contracts worth over 10 million RMB each
S Plan: Strategic Project Wins	Secure five key projects	Secure eight key projects	Secure 12 key projects
B Plan: Balanced Solution Sales	Focus on expanding business A	Focus on expanding businesses A and B	Focus on expanding businesses A and B

TABLE 4-1
THREE-YEAR MKSB PLAN

The annual plan, broken down as described above, was further decomposed into quarterly plans and weekly work reports. This way, every member of the marketing team clearly understood their weekly tasks and could promptly report on their task execution in weekly work reports. Through these reports, managers at all levels could track and supervise the implementation of the marketing strategy, ensuring its orderly progress.

After three years of diligent execution, the marketing team exceeded the targets set in the three-year plan and laid a solid foundation for the market development of the industry solutions.

Breaking down key measures into weekly work reports can serve three main functions.

First, it ensures that the key tasks of managers at all levels are centred on strategic initiatives, preventing them from falling into the trap of 'departmental fragmentation' and only focusing on their small domain.

Second, through various levels of plans and reports, managers at all levels make public commitments to dedicate sufficient time to strategic work.

Third, through systematic breakdown and frequent written communication, the entire organization can communicate, review and adjust work in a strategic, bidirectional, asynchronous manner, regardless of location and time.

This breakdown action is a routine operation in corporate management, but doing it well is not easy. Based on my experience, to truly achieve thorough breakdown and strategic implementation, managers need to pay special attention to the following influencing factors.

1. DEGREE OF MATCH OF ORGANIZATIONAL STRUCTURE

A suitable organizational structure can bring people together to collaborate, while an unsuitable structure can make team collaboration extremely difficult. Therefore, when breaking down key tasks, we need to consider the matching degree of the organizational structure, especially paying attention to the strategic alignment of managers at all levels. That is because managers' management philosophies, work experience, thinking patterns, learning abilities and behavior preferences directly influence the execution of strategic work.

For significant strategic transformations, corresponding organizational structure changes are necessary. Only in this way can strategic decisions and organizational structure positively influence each other rather than hinder or obstruct one another.

2. CONSENSUS ON STRATEGIC UNDERSTANDING

To remain competitive in an accelerating market environment, efficiently achieving organizational consensus is an essential core capability for companies. However, in a company, the focus and value demands of personnel at different levels vary. The lower the level, the more attention is often paid to short-term and local interests. For a strategy to be effectively executed, it must garner the support and commitment of the majority, making consensus among managers at all levels extremely important.

There are many methods and means to achieve consensus, such as shaping unified corporate culture and values. Most excellent companies form a long-term commitment to their values and upgrade them as needed. Dell advocates the concept that "Dell unites all of its people by valuing facts and data and establishing a belief in self-accountability." Ford Motor Company encourages the idea that "Customer satisfaction comes first, producing cars that most people can afford." Unilever's values are "to treat employees, consumers, society and our world with the highest standards of corporate behavior." Digital China's original values were "responsibility, passion, innovation, sharing," and, in the digital age, we further upgraded it to "Champion Customer Success, Create Value, Pursue Excellence, Foster Shared Growth." Another example is establishing a common vision, letting employees see hope and clearly articulating key paths, which helps people understand what needs to be done at a glance. Additionally, it is important to focus on the consensus among key groups, using the influential few to drive the majority.

3. AGILITY IN FEEDBACK AND ADJUSTMENT

Once a strategy is formulated, it must be firmly executed. However, we cannot guarantee that the plan is absolutely correct, so, during the execution process, we need to make appropriate adjustments to various measures based on feedback and changes in the external environment. Agility is an essential capability for modern enterprises and a significant challenge they face. It requires organizational members at all levels to be vigilant about potential changes in the surrounding environment. It demands that the organization can quickly allocate resources in response to rapid changes, which is not easy to achieve. That is also why I advocate for all employees at Digital China to write weekly work reports. In these reports, employees can not only provide updates on the progress of their daily work but also share their observations and thoughts for reference by superiors, subordinates and collaborative partners.

In fact, the process from strategy planning to implementation is not about how to envision it but about how to practise it. Enterprises are built through practice, not planning. We need to re-examine the strategy constantly during its implementation and continually summarize our practices. During this process, we must recognize that any endeavor involves fluctuations and reversals. We must dare to negate the negation, adopt an attitude of criticism and self-criticism, and correctly approach the exchange and clash of ideas between one another.

MAINTAIN A PROPER RHYTHM FOR STRATEGIC EXECUTION WITHOUT DEVIATION

During the execution of a strategy, many managers overlook a critical step: examining whether daily, weekly and monthly activities align with the important tasks set at the beginning of the year and ensuring that the main focus remains on the key tasks for the year.

This step is crucial, as it is an effective way to ensure that strategic execution stays on the established track.

Specifically, on the one hand, managers need to use the 'list everything' method to break down work into daily plans and weekly plans and then transform weekly plans into monthly plans, quarterly plans and annual plans. This practice involves managing time from small to large tasks. On the other hand, the formulation of daily, weekly, quarterly and yearly plans needs to be compared with strategic planning and actual implementation to determine the importance and urgency of each task. In other words, the importance of work should be assessed from large to small.

Those steps are part of the strategic adjustment process in strategic management, which involves formulating strategy and development based on the company's situation and making timely adjustments and corrections to the method of strategic execution according to actual business facts, changing business environments, new thinking and new opportunities.

In this process, managers might find that the tasks at hand have a weak relationship or even no relationship with the key objectives set at the beginning of the year. In such a case, it is necessary to adjust the work pace promptly. From this perspective, why do many strategic plans fail to be implemented and executed? It's because of the lack of review and the lack of comparison and inspection against the strategic plan. So, how should the inspection work? Who should do it? A critical responsibility of a manager is to keep prompting his employees and checking the progress of the strategy. Management is like leading an army into battle, prompting the troops to "advance at the sound of drums and retreat at the sound of gongs." In ancient China, drums were used to urge and command soldiers to advance. Generals used drumbeats to convey command signals and instructions, and managers should also 'set the rhythm' to keep everyone on track in a timely manner.

To ensure the progress of key tasks, Digital China holds meetings according to a set schedule every year. At the kick-off meeting at the beginning of the year, annual plans and key tasks are discussed to start things off. Subsequently, from weekly meetings to monthly meetings, quarterly summary meetings, semi-annual summary meetings and annual summary meetings, these meetings continually review the progress of key tasks at each stage, summarize the progress, and make timely adjustments if deviations occur. That is a planned and systematic promotion process based on strategic deployment. The organizers of these meetings are leaders at various levels, who, by adjusting the rhythm and striking the right notes, use time management and continuous iteration (listing everything) to bridge the gap between strategic planning and strategic implementation. They make timely adjustments to work direction to ensure that strategic execution stays on track.

For example, when promoting an innovative business, Digital China uses the approach of 'set the rhythm' to coordinate and advance the business.

To promote a certain innovative business, a vice president of the company took the lead in establishing a leadership team within the organizational structure as the core team for advancing the innovative business. At the same time, a specific business team was identified to undertake this strategic task fully, with corresponding responsible persons clearly designated.

At the operational mechanism level, annual targets were set, and control was maintained at different time granularities: quarterly, monthly and weekly.

- Annual: Planning and summarization, target setting, organizational structure optimization.
- Quarterly: Leadership team meetings with all members.
- Monthly: Monthly work summary reports.
- Weekly: Weekly meetings and weekly work reports from responsible persons (copied to relevant leadership team members).
- Ad-hoc: Important customer visits, special meetings.

Through actions at the different time dimensions mentioned above, the rhythm of the new business implementation process can be controlled. Whether it is through technical sharing sessions, business introduction meetings, vendor exchange meetings to stimulate sales enthusiasm, frequent customer visits during peak signing periods to assist with project closures, or shifting focus to cross-industry clients, all these actions demonstrate excellent organizational control capabilities.

Managers hold monthly and quarterly meetings to 'set the rhythm' to keep everyone on track, checking whether members have completed the tasks they should have at these time points, whether they align with strategic goals, and whether they have identified the key focus areas of their work. So, how should this 'beat' be kept to ensure it is correct and the timing is well-controlled?

In ancient China during the Spring and Autumn period, a well-known anecdote from the Battle of Changshao between the State of Lu and the State of Qi, recorded in *Zuo Zhuan – Tenth Year of Duke Zhuang*,[19] states, "In war, courage is the key. The first drumbeat boosts the soldiers' courage, the second weakens it and, by the third, their courage is gone." According to this story, the leader's choice of rhythm and timing for 'setting the rhythm' should be based on prudent observation, comprehensive analysis and accurate judgement of various factors, including changes in the strength of both sides, fluctuations in morale and changes in the external environment.

PROMOTE THE SPIRIT OF PERSEVERANCE TO BUILD STRATEGIC MOMENTUM

Having the perseverance to hammer away is an important methodology proposed by Xi Jinping. We should have the perseverance to hammer away until a task is done. More often than not, you cannot drive a nail into its right place in one go. Effective nailing requires repeated precision hammering. And to put your project in place, you have to repeat the same process of precision hammering many times. Failing that, you will end up with a shoddy project that is likely to fail at any time. Hammering nails embodies determination, tenacity and practical effort. Only with precise direction, sufficient tenacity and practical effort can nails be driven accurately, correctly and firmly.

In strategic management, we also need to promote the 'hammering away' spirit to build strategic momentum and then convert that momentum into developmental dynamism.

What is strategic momentum? Section 5, "Momentum" in *The Art of War* by Sun Tzu, states, "The onset of troops is like the rush of a torrent which will even roll stones along in its course. The quality of the decision is like the well-timed swoop of a falcon, which enables it to strike and destroy its victim. Therefore, the good fighter will be terrible at the onset and prompt in his decision. Energy may be likened to the bending of a crossbow; decision, to the releasing of a trigger." For a company, strategic momentum means creating a significant relative advantage in competition and possessing an unstoppable force in the market.

In view of building this kind of strategic momentum, the most important point is to concentrate the company's resources on the core strategy.

Why does a nail have great penetrating power and can be driven deeply into wood? It's because a nail concentrates its force on a single point, focusing its energy as much as possible. A good company is similar to a nail; it must focus its resources and forces on a single point within the expected time frame, creating focus and breakthroughs, thereby infinitely expanding its own energy.

DCITS has maintained the top market share in domestic banking core business and channel management solutions for eight consecutive years. It has now grown into a comprehensive financial technology service provider across the entire industry chain, with annual revenue exceeding 10 billion RMB. The reason for this achievement is closely related to its strategy of using flagship products as the nail, concentrating its superior forces to win key projects with important clients.

The data model management solution is an important product of DCITS. To 'nail' it into a certain joint-stock bank, the project team initiated the first domestic data modelling project. The team fully understood the project's significance to the company's financial technology strategy and deployed significant resources early on. They used an agile development model and managed the project using a Kanban approach. Ultimately, they not only overcame the performance bottleneck of entity modelling but also broke the monopoly of foreign software in the domestic data modelling market, creating a sharp tool for serving the digital transformation practices of banks.

The data asset platform solution is another competitive product developed by DCITS. To nail it into Bank N, the team concentrated on outstanding key personnel, advancing R&D and delivery simultaneously, successfully launching version 1.0 of the product, and generating considerable business for the company within the same year.

The data middle platform solution is another nail for DCITS. The company deployed its backbone staff to refine the product continuously. One subproject was particularly challenging, with an expert team working on-site for over 60 days to ensure its successful launch. Eventually, the data tools were primarily self-developed, and after the proof of concept (POC), many stability functions were iteratively improved. This solution not only gained recognition from Bank C but was also quickly replicated and promoted in the market.

So, how can we promote the spirit of perseverance?

1. FOCUS ON IMPORTANT MATTERS AND KNOW WHERE TO DRIVE THE NAILS

To achieve this, the prerequisite is to understand what constitutes important matters. Anything related to the company's strategic goals is significant. In corporate management, terms like 'goals' and 'strategy' are frequently mentioned, but many people feel that these terms have nothing to do with their work. In fact, that is not the case. Only when everyone in the company, from top to bottom, implements 'time management oriented toward strategic goals' and possesses strategic thinking and awareness can the work time invested be aligned with the strategy. It allows resources to be concentrated on achieving targets, creating pressure and achieving phased breakthroughs. Otherwise, a lot of time and human resources will be wasted.

The definition of important matters changes throughout the different stages of a company's development. Taking Digital China as an example, the first five years after the split focused on stabilizing the team and developing the business; the second five-year period aimed to overcome the challenges of service business transformation; the third five-year period focused on expanding the available capital platform; and the fourth five-year period faced the new challenge of business transformation, while also addressing internal collaboration and management issues within the corporate group based on the previous five years. The allocation of major leaders' focus and time corresponds to these key tasks. At different stages, choosing where to direct their attention embodies the essence of the 'hammering away' spirit.

2. CONCENTRATE EFFORTS ON IMPORTANT MATTERS AND CLARIFY HOW TO HAMMER THE NAILS

Without pressure and force, a nail would simply fall and penetrate nothing. However, with a press of the thumb, a nail can pierce through thick paper or even wood. That is the effect of pressure and force, concentrating all the power on a single point. Handling many tasks follows the same principle: the ability to focus power quickly is a crucial skill. A nail can be driven into wood because the target is small and the force is appropriate. Driving a nail into wood requires repeated hammering, which is a process of continuous honing and gradually overcoming difficulties step by step.

For example, a student's ability is often reflected in whether they can quickly focus their attention on one point without being distracted. Scholars in the field of cognitive science believe that attention is the foundation of learning ability and the most important intellectual factor. Some AI scientists have established attention models in the field of machine learning to simulate human intelligence in computer systems. For a person, the ability to concentrate attention determines their learning effectiveness; for a machine learning model, improving attention increases efficiency; and for a company, attention means strategic focus. The more focused a company is on its strategic core, the better the business development outcomes will be.

Continuous thinking is also necessary for important matters. In fact, thinking is a very autonomous process that doesn't require many external conditions. Whether eating, waiting for a bus, walking or running, as long as one is willing, one can concentrate on the key issues one desires to think about. When a person continuously thinks about something and forms independent and insightful opinions, they possess a certain degree of leadership. We can observe a leader's capability through their speeches. If a leader can clearly explain their key tasks without notes, it shows that they have thought about the issue for a long time and are at least a responsible leader. On the contrary, if a leader always reads from a script, it indicates that they are not confident about these matters.

STEP BACK TO SEE THE BIGGER PICTURE AND REGULARLY REVIEW AND ADJUST

When we admire an oil painting, looking at it closely, it appears blurry. Stepping back to a distance, we can understand its compositional structure. Up close, the chaotic and mottled colors distract our attention from the overall picture. By stepping back, we can see how the light and dark patches complement each other, and only from a farther distance can we grasp the entire painting's intended message.

The same principle applies to strategic execution, where being too involved clouds one's judgement, a dilemma many managers face. Based on our understanding of the objective environment and judgement of future trends, we formulate the company's strategic plan and break it down into key measures for execution. During this process, inevitable changes in the objective environment and new decision-making information will emerge. If we remain entangled in execution details without paying attention to the surrounding changes, we may be caught off guard by unexpected competitors.

Therefore, strategic management requires not only forward-looking planning and excellent execution but also continually stepping back to see the big picture. We must always maintain a macro perspective and be vigilant about significant uncertainties in economic and social development. Additionally, we need to regularly check whether the assumptions made during strategic planning are correct. If errors exist or assumptions change, the strategy must be adjusted promptly.

Over the years, I have focused on studying two patterns: one is the pattern of industry development, striving to position ahead of industry changes, such as the IT service business 15 years ago, Smart Cities ten years ago, cloud computing and big data five years ago, and now cloud-native and digital-native; the other is the pattern of internal corporate management, such as building teams, systems, processes and culture. These patterns are the essence of corporate management, taken from specific business and trivial management matters. This periodic 'stepping back to see the bigger picture' process is essentially the iterative process of corporate strategic planning and a form of periodic review.

> Since its split from Lenovo in 2000, Digital China's strategy has been adjusted and deepened every three to five years. It has transferred from the first five-year plan's 'four stages of e-commerce,' the second five-year plan's 'IT services on demand,' widely known as 'Smart Cities,' then 'cloud, big data and independent controllability' and now to 'data cloud integration and fintech.' Although our strategies have different expressions and focuses at various stages, the original strategic purposes have remained highly consistent. We have always been on the path of 'Digital China,' using cutting-edge IT technologies to provide digital services that meet the economic and social needs of the time.

This 'stepping back to see the bigger picture' process involves not only reviewing external environmental changes but also summarizing our performance. This summary includes analysing the results of a task, dissecting the work process in depth, sharing the joy of success, and summarizing and exchanging lessons learned from failures. By reviewing our goals and retracing the paths to achieve them, we gain a clear understanding of the key factors for success. Through such summary analysis, we continuously refine our goals, paths and milestones and accordingly revise our action measures to grasp the patterns and rules of business development better, continuously enhancing our organizational system's thinking ability, strengthening internal capabilities and showcasing our competitive advantages externally.

On the path to realizing the company's vision, strategic management is a process of continuous improvement and cannot be accomplished in a single effort. We need to continuously reflect, update and reshape our strategy through repeated cycles of strategic formulation, execution and iteration, which is a continuous, iterative and recurring process.

CHAPTER 5
IMPROVE PROJECT MANAGEMENT EFFICIENCY THROUGH TIME MANAGEMENT

TIME MANAGEMENT IS THE SOUL OF PROJECT MANAGEMENT

Key strategic initiatives, when planned with suitable execution timings, can be transformed, in the form of key tasks, into specific projects or project portfolios that support the realization of the strategy.

In fact, projects and project management have existed since ancient times. China's Great Wall, the Grand Canal[20] and Egypt's pyramids are all exemplary instances of engineering project management. However, the study of project management as a discipline began after World War II. The success of the Manhattan Project and the application of modern systems engineering management methods brought project management into the spotlight as a subject worth studying and made it widely recognized.

In the 1950s, the US Navy's Polaris missile nuclear submarine emergency project adopted the Program Evaluation and Review Technique (PERT), which shortened the development cycle by 20% to 25%, completing the task two years ahead of schedule. This provided a system engineering methodology for space project management. In the 1960s, the Apollo manned moon landing program achieved great success by applying the Critical Path Method (CPM) and PERT. From national defence and military industries to the aerospace field, the application scope of project management has become increasingly broad.

At the same time, with the successive establishment of the International Project Management Association (IPMA) in Europe and the Project Management Institute (PMI) in the United States, universities began to set up project management as a research discipline.

Standards, knowledge systems, certification exams and courses emerged one after another, enriching the content of the project management discipline.

As the concept of projects becomes more ingrained in people's minds, its meaning has expanded from the original engineering projects to IT projects and, further, to business and functional types of work. As long as it is not routine, daily work, we usually refer to it as a project. For example, investment and acquisition projects or certain marketing campaign projects are often mentioned.

For traditional engineering and technical projects, professional project managers have numerous reference books and certification courses to study, and they follow relatively strict project management processes. However, for those engaged in other nontechnical work, what is needed is to master the project management mindset, managing phased and temporary work efficiently as projects to deliver reliable outcomes. For daily operations, we can also break the work down into phased projects or organize campaigns, achieving phase-by-phase goals to improve the overall performance of the work.

The common definition of project management comes from PMBOK:[21] a project is a temporary endeavor undertaken to create a unique product, service or result. Project management is the application of knowledge, skills, tools and techniques to project activities to meet the project requirements. However, I prefer to think of project management as multi-objective system management based on time, with three key points: time baseline, multiple objectives and system management.

1. TIME BASELINE

One of the core boundaries of project work is time constraints, which make time management the most crucial component of project management. This element, referred to as 'temporality' in PMBOK, distinguishes project management tasks from daily operational work in enterprises. Under the time baseline, balancing quality and cost to deliver the project successfully is a key aspect of project management.

2. MULTIPLE OBJECTIVES

Multiple objectives are also a critical feature of project management. While time is an important dimension, delivering project outcomes requires balancing the triangular framework of time, cost and quality. These three elements form the 'iron triangle' or 'triple constraint' of project management. It is impossible to achieve a project that is fast, good and cheap simultaneously; most projects require trade-offs among these three elements. Selecting the most important element requires careful consideration of the true needs of the project stakeholders, which can be both explicit and implicit. For the most important aspect, we must allocate the greatest efforts to ensure its success. Maintaining this balance involves specific strategies during project execution, with numerous related methodologies and tools that won't be elaborated here.

3. SYSTEM MANAGEMENT

Project management is also a task in systems engineering. A system is defined as an integrated whole composed of interrelated, interacting and interdependent components. In *Ludwig Feuerbach and the End of Classical German Philosophy*, Friedrich Engels stated, "The great basic thought that the world is not to be comprehended as a complex of readymade things, but as a complex of processes, in which the things apparently stable no less than their mind images in our heads, the concepts, go through an uninterrupted change of coming into being and passing away, in which, in spite of all seeming accidentally and of all temporary retrogression, a progressive development asserts itself in the end." This statement, expressed philosophically, is considered the origin of system engineering.

The development of system science is almost simultaneous with project management, accompanied by the development of disciplines such as operations research and cybernetics. As human knowledge systems become increasingly complex, research into complex systems has grown, extending beyond science and technology into fields like sociology and economics. The process of project management is characterized by systemic features, comprising several components that influence one another, intertwining and coupling to form an integrated system output, which makes the project deliverable.

Executing systems engineering is not simply about holism or reductionism; it involves combining both. It requires breaking down the system into its components and understanding the relationships between them. Detailed analysis combined with a holistic view allows us to transform the system's inputs into the desired project outputs. In particular, if we neglect the systemic nature of project management and overlook its key components, it can lead to systemic risks affecting the project's outcomes.

Project management is an effective management method and is of great significance to enterprises.

First, it promotes smooth business operations. Good project management effectively allocates resources and optimizes the allocation of human, financial, material and time resources within the enterprise, ensuring project progress, guaranteeing project quality and improving work efficiency. It enables the smooth operation of various business activities, especially core business operations, and helps achieve the strategic goals of the enterprise. Moreover, during project execution, managers can identify employees' skill gaps in a timely manner and provide appropriate training, enhancing their professional qualities and improving the overall capability and market competitiveness of the enterprise.

Second, it improves internal communication within the enterprise. Effective communication between employees and departments has always been a challenge in enterprises. Effective project management can reduce the complexity of collaboration, increase transparency and ensure accountability, even when working across teams or departments, which leads to better coordination within the organization.

Third, it enables better business decision-making. Recording the progress of projects is essential in project management. This allows managers to gain deeper insights into the resources used, where they are utilized, what matters need prioritization, how to schedule time, and whether there are risks of projects going off track. This foresight enables managers to make better business decisions before problems arise.

Fourth, it enables the replication of success. How to replicate the success of one business operation to others is a challenge for many enterprises, but project management can help find the answer. By using data and experiences from previous projects, it is possible to identify areas where the team excelled and areas that needed improvement. By measuring KPIs, personalized benchmarks can be created and tracked to understand how the team executes projects individually, thereby replicating the team's success.

At Digital China, project management plays a significant role in work processes. For example, when preparing to launch a strategic, innovative business, the group assigned two highly successful managers from existing businesses as the new business leaders, but there were no related talent reserves. Therefore, building the team became the chief concern for the newly appointed recruitment director. To ensure the smooth progress of the business, the recruitment director decided to implement the recruitment work as a project, codenamed Project K. Let's look at how this project was carried out.

To manage the project effectively, the recruitment director, Mrs. Yang, analysed and summarized the key points of Project K.

Project Goals: The goals of Project K were divided into two parts: Goal A and Goal B. Goal A involved building the core team for the innovative business, requiring the identification and attraction of industry experts. Goal B consisted of assembling the execution team for the business, necessitating the bulk recruitment of professional talents to help the new business quickly reach a state of normal operation. These professional talents were divided into two levels: manager-level B1 (responsible for management duties) and regular professionals B2.

Progress Requirement: Along with the project goals, the completion timeline for the project was also specified. The schedule was very tight, requiring Goal A to be completed within six months and Goal B within two months. The reason Goal B needed to be completed first was that key positions had higher talent requirements, and matching these talents was more difficult. To help the business get on track quickly, it was necessary first to fill the professional talent positions covered by Goal B.

Task Breakdown: Like other projects, Project K required workload estimation and task breakdown. The process for onboarding a talent followed these steps: recruitment needs communication (business side and candidate side) → resume screening → talent assessment → initial interview → second interview → offer approval → entry medical examination → onboarding procedure. Estimating the recruitment workload and making a time plan involved focusing on the conversion rates for resume screening and interviews. For this, Mrs. Yang used a data funnel approach. For example, suppose a position needed to be filled with ten people within a month, with a resume qualification rate of 10% and an interview acceptance rate of 10%. Then, 100 people needed to be interviewed, and 1,000 resumes needed to be recommended. That implied a daily recommendation of 50 resumes, weekly interviews of 25 people, and issuing three offers per week (with some redundancy to account for offer rejections).

Project Team: Faced with the challenge of a tight schedule and heavy tasks, the traditional model of HR handling the recruitment for one business group (BG) was no longer feasible. Mrs. Yang thought of forming a virtual team. By establishing an innovative talent acquisition project group, recruitment personnel from headquarters were brought in to participate in the early and peak stages of Project K. This approach allowed for the collective advancement of the talent acquisition project without significantly impacting the recruitment progress of other business units.

Personnel Allocation: After multiple rounds of communication and coordination, the project group was formed, consisting of six members. Recruitment director Mrs. Yang served as the project manager, responsible for overall project advancement and full-cycle recruitment for Goal A. The new business recruitment lead, Mrs. Lin, was responsible for the full-cycle recruitment of B1-level talents and acted as the primary contact with the innovative business team, handling tasks like communicating requirements and pushing resumes while also assisting

Mrs. Yang with some A-level talent screening. The four virtual project team members from headquarters were responsible for the full-cycle recruitment of B2-level talents while ensuring the progress of their original recruitment work.

Project Process Management: To ensure project outcomes, Mrs. Yang implemented strict process control. She held daily project progress meetings at 6 pm to track everyone's daily progress. If any issues arose, they would be addressed immediately, leaving no problems unresolved overnight.

Challenges and Countermeasures: Several challenges were encountered during recruitment. For instance, key position candidates were scarce, even with open recruitment channels, especially through headhunters, but candidates were still limited. Later, suitable candidates were found through targeted talent mapping. However, convincing them to leave established companies for a startup business posed significant concerns. Mrs. Yang overcame this by working with department heads to highlight business strengths and successfully attract the necessary talent.

Professional position recruitment also faced resistance, such as interruptions in face-to-face interviews due to the pandemic. Mrs. Yang adopted online video interview modules to enhance efficiency. Another issue was poor recruitment channel performance in local areas, which was resolved by opening local talent websites and promoting them prominently, achieving better talent attraction.

Project Execution Results: After six months of effort, the project team completed all tasks and achieved all expected outcomes. All recruitment for the innovative business was completed by the project team members themselves, without using headhunters, saving the company millions in recruitment channel costs.

Project Review: In reviewing the entire project process, two key success factors emerged.

First, process management ensured timely information synchronization, coordination and feedback from different perspectives, resolving issues promptly. It included daily updates from remote locations, daily progress tracking for the project team and weekly recruitment progress syncs with business departments.

Second, different strategies were used for other recruitment needs. For Goal A, targeting key positions, a slow but steady approach was used, focusing on top industry companies to recruit core team members successfully. For Goal B, targeting bulk professional positions, efficient coordination within the virtual project team and a data funnel model enabled rapid progress.

Six months later, the innovative project recruitment entered a normal operational phase, and the successful project management provided valuable experience for both the project team and the company. This experience can be replicated for future projects with urgent needs, helping the business get on track quickly.

In project management, the goals and content of time management mainly focus on allocating time resources to various project activities and controlling the project's progress and completion. Generally speaking, projects often have very challenging time targets and schedules. Many projects' ultimate commercial goals are also time-related. For example, the vast majority of new product development projects require meeting market time windows. Therefore, effectively utilizing time, a unique resource, is key to project success, and time management is the most crucial aspect of project management.

PLAN TIME WELL TO ENSURE PROJECT PROGRESS

Since projects must deliver results within the specified time frame, planning how time is used becomes very important. We need to know how much time is spent on what activities and what results these activities produce, which will ultimately contribute to the overall project outcomes.

- Break down work tasks;
- Assess resources required for tasks;
- Prioritize tasks; and
- Create work plans and schedule progress.

Let's look at each of these four aspects in detail.

1. BREAKING DOWN WORK TASKS

Breaking down work tasks involves decomposing the work and final deliverables required for the project into executable activities and measurable phased outcomes, forming a Work Breakdown Structure (WBS). It is best to list all tasks in a clear task list and distribute them to each member of the project team so everyone understands how much work needs to be done.

This breakdown is not a simple linear decomposition (e.g., dividing 10 million RMB of profit among five sales managers) but rather a breakdown considering the relevant background factors of the project. These factors include project type, requirements, work processes, organizational structure, etc. The basis for the breakdown can consist of but is not limited to, the physical or functional structure of the deliverables, project subgoals, implementation process, project distribution area, organization and functions.

The process of breaking down tasks should follow three principles. First is the goal-oriented principle: the breakdown should focus on work outputs, then align these outputs with work tasks (referred to as activities in PMBOK) rather than directly listing task content. Second is the MECE principle (mutually exclusive, collectively exhaustive): the decomposed tasks should be nonoverlapping and comprehensive. Of course, since projects often change their course, we should also follow the principle of 'detailed near-term, broad long-term' to save planning time.

2. ASSESSING RESOURCES REQUIRED FOR TASKS

For the decomposed work tasks, we need to evaluate the required resources, such as workforce, time, materials and funds. The most relevant aspect of progress is time estimation, which is also the most challenging aspect of task evaluation. Experienced managers can make more accurate time estimates. However, if we lack sufficient experience to estimate time resources for a new project, we should leave some buffer in our workload estimation to allow for future adjustments.

There are three commonly used methods for estimating the time required for tasks, similar to cost estimation:
- Analogous estimation: This involves using similar past projects for reference. Essentially, this is a form of expert judgement, also known as top-down estimation.
- Function point analysis: Also known as bottom-up estimation, this method involves detailed breakdowns of the project, estimating the cost for each activity, and summing them up to get the total time or cost.

- Three-point estimation: This involves estimating from three perspectives: the most optimistic, the most likely and the most pessimistic scenarios.

When mid-level and senior managers conduct evaluations, they should carefully listen to the opinions of front-line managers. Their extensive experience is a valuable asset to the company and a part of the organization's knowledge base. Digital China is committed to building a digital platform, one of the purposes of which is to consolidate these knowledge assets and allow the real data accumulated during project operations to assist in decision-making gradually.

3. PRIORITIZING TASKS

To prioritize tasks, managers need to analyse the importance, urgency and sequence of tasks, particularly their time dependencies, to achieve the highest efficiency under all given project constraints. Hua Luogeng's coordination method is a feasible approach; we can use a dependency graph to examine the relationships between tasks and optimize their arrangement visually.

It is important to note that during the actual execution of projects, a common issue often arises: the person responsible for a subproject or subtask may lack a clear understanding of the position of their part within the overall project and other tasks that precede or follow their subtask. If this person encounters other more urgent and important matters, they may easily postpone the subtask they are responsible for in the main project, leading to a series of delays in the main project's tasks. To avoid such issues, managers need to communicate thoroughly with the heads of each subtask, reach a consensus and clarify the position and responsibilities of each task. Then, when tasks are pushed, they will be done proactively rather than making the coordination plan a mere formality.

4. SCHEDULE WORK PLANS

Once the task content, required resources, and task priorities have been determined, we can plan and schedule the overall project work based on the information above. There are many ways to present this schedule, including common formats such as Gantt charts, milestone charts and network logic diagrams. However, regardless of the format, the core content is the representation of project tasks over time.

When arranging the work plan, two key points must be considered. First, there must be a commitment from the participants; decisions cannot be made without their involvement, as this would be detrimental to future project execution. Second, the schedule should be tight yet achievable, ensuring no idle time while guaranteeing the smooth completion of the project.

Having completed the above steps, it may seem that the project is now under control. However, adjusting plans during project execution is often more challenging.

Completing the project on time with quality standards is the common expectation of every manager, yet delays frequently occur. How can time be reasonably allocated within the project time constraints to ensure timely completion? The measures taken by Digital China in response to delays in a software project might offer some insights.

In 2020, Digital China, along with four other companies, jointly participated in the construction of a certain software project. For this, the company assigned one product manager, three front-end development engineers, two back-end development engineers and two test engineers to the site.

Digital China joined at the end of May, coinciding with the planning period for the second major version 2.0. After version 1.0 went live, work began on developing version 2.0. Version 1.0 experienced a one-month delay at launch, which led to client dissatisfaction with the project team and strained the partnership. For version 2.0, throughout the planning, development and launch stages, the project team faced the following issues.

In addition to a set deadline for the 2.0 launch, they also had to manage a strained client relationship. Moreover, the development schedule was significantly delayed, presenting a dual challenge. Compared to the severe external situation, the team found that internal conflicts within the project group were even more challenging. As the project group consisted of multiple companies, and each company's project members were temporarily assigned, they faced numerous difficulties in communication, coordination and responsibility division. Every day, each person spent 90% of their time in meetings and syncing information, leaving only 10% of the time for actual work, which led to frequent arguments and quarrels in the office. Professional tasks had to be completed during evenings and weekends, with members blaming and complaining about each other, a situation that persisted for two months after the formation of the project team.

The project manager had only created a rough schedule for reporting to the client. From the perspective of the entire project team, there was no detailed schedule for the project tasks; all members only knew that the project was scheduled to launch on 30 June. However, nobody knew when requirement confirmation, development or internal testing would start. The requirement documents were revised repeatedly without confirmation from the client, leaving little time for subsequent tasks.

Because the requirements were not confirmed, user interface (UI) testing and development work were always in a semi-started state. Whenever the project manager pushed for progress, project members began to complain. The UI designer lamented, "I know the launch time is tight, but the requirements keep changing. I've adjusted a page four times in one day, worked until 3 am last night and was told to change it back by noon the next day. When will this end?" The tester said, "There are over 300 test cases for version 2. When a requirement changes, I have to adjust the test cases accordingly. Half of my time is spent modifying test cases. At this rate, I might as well sleep in the office instead of going home."

In the chaotic state of the project, the project manager organized a discussion with the on-site leaders of each company. They first investigated why the requirement confirmation process was stuck. It was found that a primary product manager, aiming to showcase herself, was arbitrarily adding requirements. Therefore, the project manager decided to remove her from the project group and replace her with another product manager.

Next was the project scheduling. They reviewed the dependencies and sequence of tasks. The internal project group considered the number of teams and integrated factors such as resource allocation, task interdependencies and prerequisites. For the external project group, they thought about the coordination, expertise and progress of each client department. They also factored in the dependencies between the internal and external project groups.

After the project manager reviewed all tasks, relevant personnel estimated the completion time for activities based on factors affecting the project schedule (project scope, resource conditions, personnel capabilities and environment) and then created the schedule. During schedule estimation, senior experts from each team analysed and evaluated, referencing previous similar projects, and included a buffer time to address risks such as team turnover and delays in some offline processes.

As a result, the project team established an online plan board. Based on the content of the current iteration version and the 30 June launch date, they created a schedule and published it to the entire project team.

After executing this model for a while, progress and quality were effectively controlled. Despite a delay in the version 2.0 launch by half a month due to some of the team members' failure to meet deadlines, there was a significant improvement compared to the project's initial stage.

After the launch, the project manager organized a review meeting to address new issues that emerged. During the meeting, it was unanimously agreed to implement daily stand-up meetings to address delays caused by individual members. At 10 am every day, each team would have one representative

attend the stand-up meeting in the conference room, each limited to one minute to answer three questions:
1. What did you do yesterday?
2. What are you planning to do today?
3. Are there any difficulties, or do you need assistance?

At the first meeting, half the members were unprepared for the one-minute limit and were interrupted halfway. Everyone learned from the experience and prepared their reports in advance for the second meeting, ensuring that all reports were completed within the one-minute limit.

Daily meetings are generally limited to ten minutes. Two ways to control meeting time are: first, hold stand-up meetings where participants communicate while standing, reducing idle talk and topic divergence; second, answer only the three questions mentioned above, avoid discussion of issues and prevent finger-pointing and blame-shifting during the meeting.

Following these measures, project team members collaborated closely, and the chaotic situation was not repeated. Subsequent iterations were steadily launched according to the schedule, and the project team regained the client's recognition.

In enterprises, many projects need to be completed as quickly as possible, and any time loss in one phase can negatively impact other phases, potentially causing the entire project to be delayed. That is why effective time planning is crucial: by managing project time well, you are essentially managing project progress effectively.

MANAGE STAKEHOLDERS AND THEIR EXPECTATIONS: SLOW MEANS FAST

Once time planning is done well, the next step is to enter the project implementation phase. Ideally, if the plan is reasonable and there are no significant changes, the project can be delivered smoothly by strictly following the plan. However, project implementation is often not ideal. Various issues may arise during execution: low cooperation from client participants, client dissatisfaction with phased deliverables, employee turnover, difficulty in meeting new client requirements, challenges in mobilizing resources from internal departments, resistance from senior employees, acceptance and payment difficulties, and so on.

Problems inevitably arise. How do we address them?

By analysing these issues, it is clear that common project problems are often related to people. If we can properly manage these people-related issues or foresee problems and nip them in the bud, reducing conflicts as much as possible, project time and progress will be more controllable.

Conflicts are merely inconsistencies in expectations, information asymmetry or a combination of both before becoming conflicts. These inconsistencies may arise from different roles or perspectives. In project management, managing stakeholders involves understanding these different perspectives and narrowing inconsistencies and asymmetries through appropriate communication methods, frequency and content.

Generally, project stakeholders include sponsors (those who fund the project), clients and users (those who use the project's outcomes), vendors (suppliers), business partners, the project team (internal teams related to the project) and functional personnel (department staff who provide technical and resource support for the project). Here, we will focus on three parties with the most significant stakes: the client, the team and the leader.

1. MANAGING THE CLIENT

When working on business to business (B2B) projects, we often deal with multiple teams, decision chains and stakeholders within the client organization. We need to identify everyone on the project's key decision chain, understand their expectations, and be well-informed so that we can manage our actions effectively. It is especially important to gain the support of the final decision maker; direct communication is best, but if not possible, ensure smooth information flow. Note that the final decision-maker is not necessarily the highest-ranking person but the one with the authority to make direct decisions. Managing the client involves two main points: understanding and meeting the client's needs and controlling their expectations. The former improves client experience, while the latter reduces client expectations. The difference between these two factors determines the client satisfaction that affects our delivery results.

2. MANAGING THE TEAM

The project implementation team is the project manager's responsibility. The process of team management in this project is a typical application of the planning, organizing, coordinating and controlling functions discussed in Chapter 2. In addition to the general management principles of clear division of labor, team motivation and leading by example, the challenge of managing a project-oriented team compared to operational management lies mainly in the temporary nature of the project.

The temporary nature means that the project has a time limit, and the team composition is unstable. Given these characteristics, it becomes crucial to form the right team based on project goals, identifying the key skills needed and matching them with members' strengths to maximize synergy. This approach not only provides team members with a sense of achievement but also helps create a morale-driven atmosphere where results are achieved and responsibilities are met.

3. MANAGING THE LEADERSHIP

In project management, the project manager must handle upward management toward the leadership. These leaders may include business line leaders or heads of project groups or portfolios. Upward management in project-oriented work includes three main aspects: synchronizing project expectations with the leaders, obtaining their commitment and authorization, and assigning tasks to the leaders.

An often-overlooked aspect is synchronizing both parties' project expectations. It involves understanding the leaders' expectations for the project and making them aware of the project's importance and value through timely and reasonable reporting. A more challenging task is to manage the leaders' time by flexibly coordinating their resources and involving them in customer interactions, project reviews and team meetings. These activities can significantly drive the project's progress.

A project manager grows from a novice to a seasoned professional by practising and refining their skills in managing 'people' issues. The more experiences one goes through, the stronger their problem-solving abilities become. The principles mentioned above serve only as guidelines; true capabilities are honed through practical experience.

DCITS won the overall architecture consulting project for Company M. The client hoped to plan the future blueprint for the company's information system through this project. The goal was to establish a unified information system across the entire company, with unified standards and specifications and a unified construction approach. The time requirement was six months.

Due to internal disagreements within the client's organization regarding the construction plan, the project progressed slowly. After understanding the issue, the project manager identified the main stakeholders of the project and clarified the leaders' demands through communication, accelerating the project's progress. Because some time had been lost, the project manager negotiated with the client to plan and deliver the overall project in phases. After repeated communications, a consensus was reached. Subsequently, the project proceeded smoothly. The entire project team ultimately completed the project work on schedule, with high quality and within the planned timeline.

Although we have focused on technical project management in this section, project management is truly both a work philosophy and a methodological system that can be applied to almost any type of work. Colleagues responsible for brand management organize a market event, HR colleagues promote campus recruitment, and finance colleagues undertake asset restructuring. All these tasks can be managed using project management methods. In practice, Digital China advances its annual key tasks by using project management methods in terms of setting goals and milestones and managing the project process, thus yielding positive results.

MAKE GOOD USE OF VISUALIZATION TOOLS IN PROJECT TIME MANAGEMENT

In project time management, the use of visualization tools can yield twice the result with half the effort. Visualization tools can display task breakdowns, assignments and execution progress online and in real time, greatly improving the efficiency of communication among project team members.

Historically, the development of modern project management has been inseparable from the advancement of information technology. Since the 1950s, the development and application of various software have provided direct assistance in improving project management efficiency. Over decades of development, project management software has evolved from early single-machine software deployed on mainframes and minicomputers to internet-based collaborative software and the currently popular cloud services, greatly enhancing enterprise project management capabilities.

Visualization tools have also played a significant role in the development of Digital China.

Digital China's digital middle platform is a key focus in the company's digital transformation process. To reduce the time friction cost in team communication and cultivate a unified work habit among all core team members, the person in charge promoted the use of two tools within the team: an online shared calendar and a knowledge-sharing space.

The online shared calendar may seem simple, but it is very effective for team time management. Suppose all team members' schedules are integrated into the calendar and shared. There would be no need to call or message each person individually to schedule a meeting, thus significantly improving the overall team coordination efficiency.

Online collaborative documents can synchronize content that needs to be shared within the team, and are mostly used for meeting minutes and task allocation. It can structure the decisions generated from meeting minutes to identify tasks, responsible persons and deadlines, allowing team members to track and manage task progress through structured data. Compared to ordinary single-machine meeting minutes, online collaborative documents offer functions for recording, publishing, supervising and monitoring tasks, providing direct management for task progression. Of course, when using these shared file functions, it is important to set permissions to prevent the leakage of trade secrets.

Through the effective use of these tools, the digital middle platform team quickly moved from initial confusion to a state of high-efficiency collaboration, making significant contributions to the company's digital transformation efforts.

Some effective visualization tools for reference:

1. GANTT CHART

The Gantt chart, a type of bar chart, is the most widely used and influential visualization tool in project management. It was developed by engineer Henry Laurence Gantt in 1910. Its main presentation format establishes project tasks on the vertical axis and time on the horizontal axis, using bars of different colors to represent planned and actual progress. It is displayed within this quadrant area to clarify the start and end dates of project-related tasks, including resources, milestones, tasks and dependencies.

The Gantt chart can clearly and intuitively display the tasks that need to be completed, the time required, and the interrelationships between various resources. It also allows team members to view the relationship between their work and others. Therefore, the Gantt chart is very suitable for tracking project progress. In addition, it can display progress, resources, constraints and other relevant scheduling information.

There are many ways to create Gantt charts. We can use Excel (see Figure 5-1) or project management software like Microsoft Project. Business Intelligence (BI) software also provides Gantt chart templates, such as Power BI, Smart eVision and Tableau.

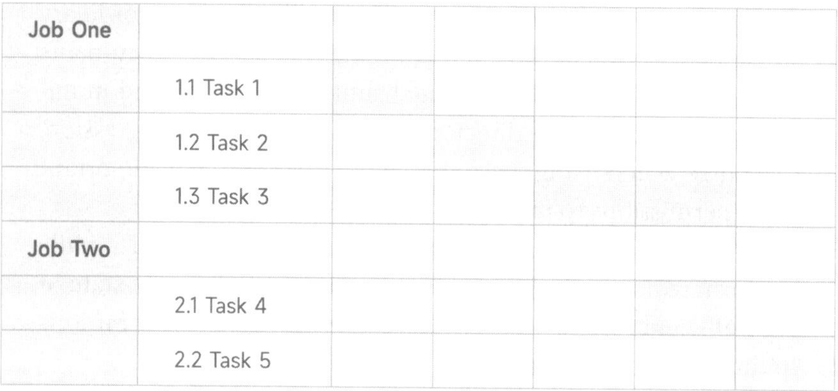

Job One						
	1.1 Task 1					
	1.2 Task 2					
	1.3 Task 3					
Job Two						
	2.1 Task 4					
	2.2 Task 5					

FIGURE 5-1
EXAMPLE OF A GANTT CHART

2. WORK BREAKDOWN STRUCTURE (WBS)

As mentioned earlier, in the time-planning phase of project management, work should be decomposed into a Work Breakdown Structure (WBS). It is not only a necessary task in the early stages of project management but also a commonly used tool.

WBS is oriented toward deliverable project outcomes. It decomposes the project according to certain principles, breaking it down into tasks, further into individual activities and finally assigning these activities to each person's daily tasks until no further breakdown is possible (see Figure 5-2).

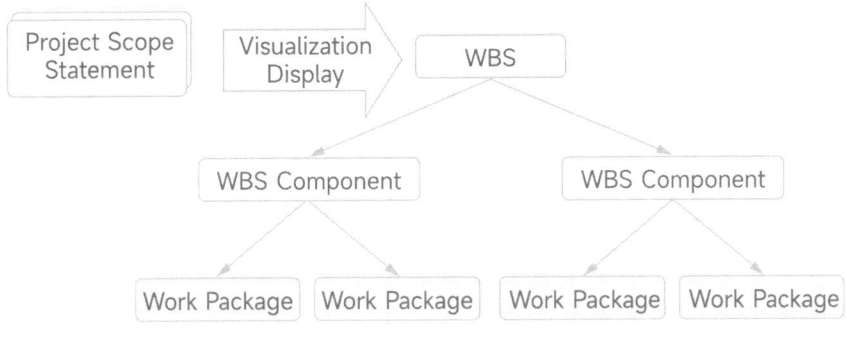

FIGURE 5-2
EXAMPLE OF WBS BREAKDOWN

The WBS is the foundation for various project tasks, such as schedule planning, resource requirements, cost budgeting, procurement planning and risk management. There are many tools and software available for executing WBS, such as Excel, Visio and MindManager, as well as specialized project management software. The challenge lies in understanding the project's actual work. Only with sufficient expertise can the work be decomposed logically and reasonably.

3. SWIMLANE DIAGRAM

A swimlane diagram is a type of UML[22] Activity Diagram, also known as a cross-functional flowchart (see Figure 5-3). It is derived from traditional flowcharts but adds different departments, execution entities or functional areas to the horizontal and vertical coordinates. This allows for an intuitive display of the process's respective units, helping stakeholders from different roles in the project understand the business logic of other parts.

Similar to WBS decomposition, swimlane diagrams can typically be created using software like Visio or StarUML, as well as project management software like JIRA or ONES.

During the project management process, these visualization tools can help team members quickly synchronize information and reach a consensus. Beyond these specific diagram tools, there are software applications for managing individual projects and systems for managing company and departmental projects. These tools have played a significant role in enterprise management.

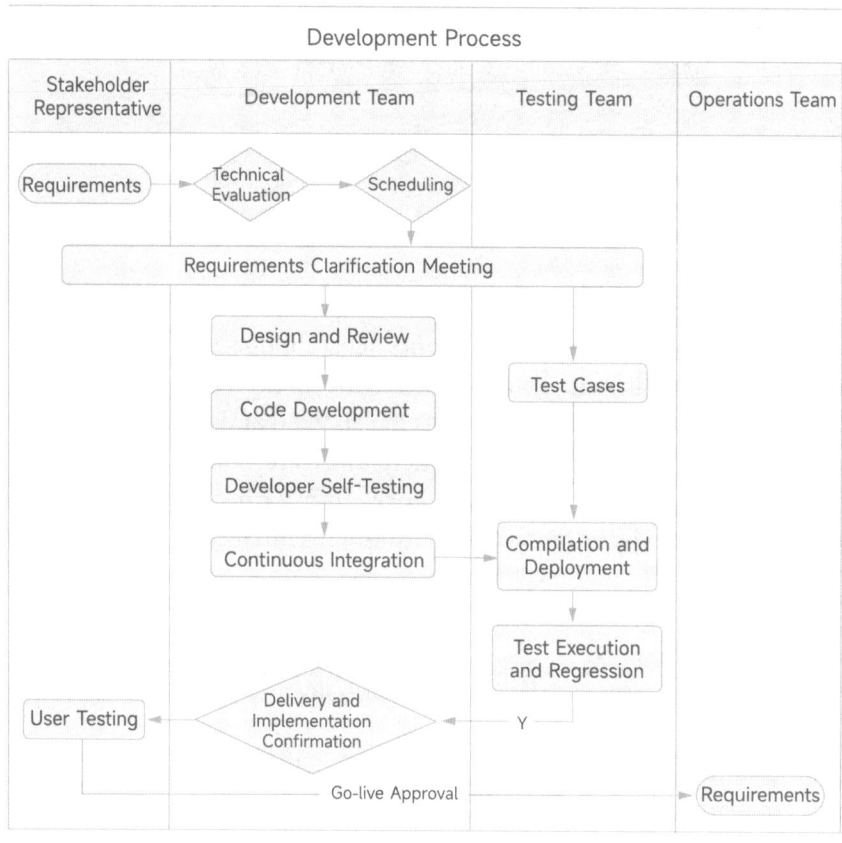

FIGURE 5-3
EXAMPLE OF A SWIMLANE DIAGRAM

For example, Digital China's collaborative development tools have greatly assisted the efficient management of the OA team.

The digital technology department is responsible for the company's overall digital technologies. One of its routine key tasks is managing the collaborative OA system. Digital China's collaborative OA platform has been in operation for nearly 20 years, supporting hundreds of applications and comprehensively sustaining the company's daily management operations. Under the strategic backdrop of the company's comprehensive cloud transformation, the collaboration efficiency across departments needs to be further improved, and the collaborative OA platform urgently needs optimization and improvement in both business processes and technical frameworks. In this improvement process, the collaborative OA project team must, on the one hand, cooperate with business departments to implement or rebuild business processes and, on the other hand, upgrade the technical framework of the collaborative OA applications, migrating from the old platform to the new one.

To ensure the smooth implementation of the team's key tasks, the department provided strong support for development resources. However, since the end of 2018, due to increased workloads and changes in team composition, the collaborative OA team encountered several issues:

- Shortage of development resources for the old platform: The collaborative OA system was repeatedly split due to business splits, and the construction of Digital China's financial shared service centre required process modifications for multiple old platform financial applications. As a result, there was a significant increase in related maintenance and development needs compared to the same period in previous years. Meanwhile, engineers for the old platform were gradually being replaced by new platform engineers, leading to severe delays in meeting the demands for the old platform.
- The increase in daily parallel tasks has intensified the difficulty of resource allocation and management. With a high daily maintenance workload, numerous urgent requirements, and multiple key projects running in parallel, every task seemed important, and clients considered their needs urgent. Efficiently allocating limited resources to various tasks became a new challenge.

- Delayed internal team communication and risk management: Due to an increase in team members, numerous parallel tasks, and remote management (in Beijing and Wuhan), there were frequent delays or omissions in progress reporting and handling results for specific tasks. It hindered the timely identification of issues, resulting in missing early improvement opportunities.
- The work volume statistics and evaluation for team members lacked an objective basis. In the company's DT management change process, engineers filled out the work volume in one go after the implementation was completed. Due to the lack of process management tools, evaluators could not obtain the actual time invested and daily work details for each task by the evaluated person, making it difficult to assess their work capability and performance objectively.

At this time, the digital technology department began promoting the internal use of a project and task-tracking management tool platform. The collaborative OA team took advantage of this opportunity to implement time management methodology effectively using this tool. They primarily executed the following actions.

1. Correctly 'listing everything': Classify all work based on the team's work content characteristics (modules) and manage each classification by breaking down all work into task lists of different granularities.
2. Reasonably balancing arrangements: Team managers confirm and mark the priority of related tasks in the system, dynamically adjusting the time requirements and resource allocation for key tasks. It ensures the timely handling of urgent tasks and the gradual implementation of key work within the existing resources.
3. Review and summary: Team members report their daily work content and workload under the corresponding tasks in the system (daily work report function). Team managers can see the reported content in real time through system email notifications and can always monitor the progress of key tasks through customized statistical reports. It allows them to promptly identify problems,

analyse causes, find solutions and continuously improve the team's management model within the system.

After six months of using and adjusting the system, the collaborative OA team has gradually alleviated or solved the previously mentioned issues. The results show that the team has transitioned from a personnel-based management approach to a project and task-based management one. On the basis of team consensus, all recognized work has been broken down into standard tasks, significantly improving the efficiency of information synchronization within the team. Additionally, resource allocation has shifted from being vague to precise, and all tasks can be effectively tracked and controlled from a time management perspective, reducing reliance on individual task executors. Furthermore, due to the timeliness and accuracy of task and time tracking, project cost estimates have become more accurate, and employee evaluations can be more objective.

It is important to note that when selecting specific visualization tools, the latest is not necessarily the best. Choices should be based on the actual application in their industry and organization, as well as their own needs. The most suitable tool is the most useful one.

CHAPTER 6

BUILD ORGANIZATIONAL LEADERSHIP THROUGH TIME MANAGEMENT

MANAGE TIME TO ENHANCE ORGANIZATIONAL LEADERSHIP

When we delve deeper into the concept of time management, we realize that what seems like straightforward time management is not just about strategic management and project management but encompasses the entire organization. Management is never piecemeal or partial; it is systematic and holistic.

Through various time management tools, we emphasize the decomposition of strategies layer by layer at the organizational level and align key tasks to enhance organizational consistency. Doing this includes consistency in strategic goals, values, management language, key tasks and communication methods. By constraining these key aspects, we create synergy.

We all know that it is challenging to find a universal key to business success. However, many entrepreneurs agree that organizational consistency plays a crucial role in the development of an enterprise. With organizational consistency, an enterprise can improve efficiency and effectiveness from a higher perspective. When an organization unifies its thoughts and enhances efficiency on a larger scale, its combat effectiveness will be significantly improved, and this execution capability will eventually translate into benefits and profits.

Organizational consistency directly manifests in the enhancement of leadership within an enterprise. To some extent, this is the greatest value that time management creates for organizational management.

Why is leadership so important? Whether it is a country, a company or a department, every organization needs outstanding leaders.

Only exceptional leaders can continuously elevate an organization to greater heights. However, the key issue is how we can find such exceptional leaders. Or how can we cultivate such exceptional leaders?

Over the past 40 years, China's economic development has been rapid and enterprises, as market entities, have always faced complex external situations, especially in the present, where issues are particularly complicated. These complex issues are both challenges and opportunities. They are, for example, the changes in market supply and demand brought about by new trends in globalization, the changes in work methods brought about by the COVID-19 pandemic, and the industrial changes brought about by technological developments such as cloud computing and cloud-native, big data and digital-native, blockchain, the metaverse and artificial intelligence.

Although Digital China has always been engaged in digital products and services, it is still not considered a digital-native enterprise. Facing such a complex external environment, how can we achieve the transformation from a nondigital-native enterprise to a digital-native enterprise? How can we establish an organizational form that adapts to rapid technological changes? How can we seize the opportunities brought by the current dramatic changes? How can we transform management processes and models that were suitable for the 70s and 80s to adapt to the young teams now composed of the 90s and 00s?

To address all these challenges, we need to cultivate outstanding leaders. Our core cadres must shoulder this mission, one bestowed upon us by history, by the times and by our more than 20,000 employees. We must do it well.

What exactly is leadership?

Titles, positions or roles do not automatically create leadership. Leadership is not simply about obedience; it is about guiding everyone to a common destination. It manifests through the interactions between leaders and team members and can be observed at various levels and in different fields. Leadership exists around us: in company management, in government, in the military, on the sports field, in classrooms and even in every small family. It is the core of accomplishing everything effectively.

Everyone has a different understanding of leadership. If we try to define it comprehensively, there are many possibilities: leadership is the ability to influence others and the team to achieve set goals; the essence of leadership is influence; leadership is trust and belief. However defined, it is never complete and cannot unify everyone's views on it. Therefore, I prefer to describe it by answering the question, "What should we do to develop leadership within an organization?" At the same time, I want to emphasize that I am referring to organizational leadership within an organization, not just personal leadership.

Based on this idea, I have attempted to summarize a four-element model of leadership (see Figure 6-1).

FIGURE 6-1
THE FOUR-ELEMENT MODEL OF LEADERSHIP

Momentum, communication, incentive mechanism and discipline are the core elements of organizational leadership.

Leadership requires the ability to guide, which necessitates high momentum. Why do subordinates follow superiors? Because superiors have greater momentum, and subordinates must execute received instructions. If subordinates are unwilling to perform, superiors need to reflect on how to increase their momentum. A role model possesses momentum because personal practice is the most persuasive, influential and inspiring. Through long-term training and accumulation in business, leaders form professional capabilities, understand the overall situation better, assign tasks more professionally and provide excellent operational suggestions at critical points, which is key to gaining genuine respect. An essential aspect of momentum comes from ideals and views of the future. For example, how do we envision the future development of technology? What changes will occur in supporting infrastructure? How will it be applied in various industries? Based on these judgements, we find the company's future position and drive the entire company in that direction, demonstrating vision and momentum.

With momentum, communication is needed, and various communication methods are used to achieve consensus. Momentum comes from views of the future. Then, this belief must be conveyed to gain collective agreement. Team combat effectiveness, like the principles of mechanics, requires aligned force directions to form a synergy; otherwise, they will counteract each other. Within a team, consensus leads to resonance, generating powerful strength. As a leader, after determining the direction, choosing the method of communication is crucial. There are many ways of conducting this, such as training, meetings, one-on-one communication and corporate websites. The purpose of these methods is to convey directional and strategic information, allowing everyone to understand and reach a consensus.

An incentive mechanism is required to build a good organization. People's behavior cannot rely on being constantly prodded; instead, everyone should feel willing to spontaneously and automatically do things within the system, integrating the organization's goals with their own. This part of leadership requires us to design such mechanisms.

Finally, an organization must have discipline and very clear constraints. The significant difference between an individual and an organization is constraint. Whether an organization has constraints is a manifestation of its leadership. Every organization needs discipline. Even a kindergarten must teach children to follow the rules and develop good habits. Sitting still, not speaking out of turn, and concentrating on listening to the teacher, beginning in five to ten minutes and then going to 20 minutes, and eventually being able to sit attentively for 40 minutes, is a form of constraint.

A truly outstanding organization should not rely solely on individual leaders but rather on a systematically constructed institutional framework. This framework includes both positive incentive mechanisms and negative disciplinary constraints. If the institutional structure is reasonable, scientifically configured, procedurally rigorous and effectively constrained, it can form the organizational leadership necessary to ensure the organization operates in the right direction. Conversely, a flawed system can weaken organizational leadership and even have adverse effects. Transitioning from 'rule of man' to 'rule of law' is essential for the growth and strengthening of an enterprise.

Based on the aforementioned four-element model, let's delve into how to establish momentum, how to communicate and reach consensus, how to build mechanisms and how to clarify discipline.

BUILD MOMENTUM AND BELIEVE IN 'THE POWER OF BELIEVING'

To lead is to guide or to direct. But where does it lead to? It is to lead to a place of belief. Therefore, the momentum of leadership lies in being able to lead the team in believing in the power of believing. How can this be achieved?

This requires managers to have a strategic vision, a comprehensive understanding of the company's future development path and a thorough consideration of major issues that may arise during development. They must effectively control risks and crises and guide everyone to find a pattern that maximizes each person's value, which is crucial.

Why is momentum important? In some sense, momentum is, first and foremost, the leader's awareness. Can you show your colleagues what you see? If you can only see it yourself but cannot make others see or believe it, you cannot influence them.

Where does momentum come from? First, it comes from authority, especially the clear authority of a position. It is the condition that ensures momentum. Everyone in the company has their position, with levels such as presidents, general managers, directors, etc. These different levels of positions mean different responsibilities and corresponding authorities. Many emphasize nonauthoritative leadership, encouraging boundaryless equality and freedom, but I believe we should not avoid positional authority. From any perspective, positional authority is the most fundamental guarantee of leadership momentum. Superiors have management responsibilities and authority over subordinates because they bear responsibility.

Subordinates can express different opinions to superiors but must execute the orders given.

We often hear managers complain that their subordinates do not listen to them. The first thing to reflect on is what leadership issues might be causing this problem. How should it be resolved? Complaints do not solve problems; we must solve the problem. Only by ensuring this most basic level of positional authority compliance can the organization operate efficiently. If even this cannot be achieved, then one cannot be considered a leader of the organization.

In fact, the authority that comes with a position does not always bring about authority and unconditional compliance. For instance, I often face challenges myself. If I want to organize a meeting, and someone requests leave for a certain reason, should I approve it or not? Approving it might suggest a lack of authority – if the chairman cannot gather everyone for a meeting, what authority do they have? However, disapproval might raise other issues. Sometimes, it's an urgent personal matter, and not approving it may seem unkind. Sometimes, it's to meet a client, and not approving it might make us appear overly bureaucratic, hindering business operations. Such dilemmas frequently arise.

That is one of the reasons why we emphasize time management. If we can manage everyone's time well, avoid such conflicts and hold the meeting successfully, we can achieve collaboration and reflect the leader's authority. It may seem like a small matter, but effective time management can be a process of establishing authority. If we disregard objective laws and forcefully disrupt others' schedules, the meeting cannot be held, and we end up undermining ourselves.

We must understand that, even as leaders, we cannot arbitrarily disrupt everyone's normal work. For instance, excessive meetings lead to very low overall efficiency. How can we ensure everyone's work rhythm while achieving coordination and protecting the leader's momentum? It is an art of management that requires balance.

How do we build momentum? It requires us to harness four types of power:

1. THE POWER OF EXAMPLES – ESTABLISH AUTHORITY THROUGH PRACTICAL EXPERIENCE

As a leader, how high should the standards for oneself be? If a leader applies double standards internally and externally, being strict with others and lenient with themselves, it is clear that momentum cannot be established. In fact, the opposite is true. One must become a role model to gain momentum because a leader's momentum is not only reflected in their high position but also in whether everyone truly respects them. Three levels of capabilities need to be trained to achieve such momentum so that one can have radiating influence and deterrent power when making decisions and giving commands.

On the first level, a leader must have professional expertise. He must be an expert in their field. The prerequisite for leadership is proficiency in the business. If a leader is not competent, they cannot make sound judgements, let alone lead the team to victory. For example, if someone cannot close a major deal in sales, they will not gain the respect of their team if put in charge of sales. Therefore, a leader must first become a field expert, able to identify the essence and patterns of tasks and find effective ways to succeed. This process of becoming an expert requires accumulation and cannot be a shortcut. Additionally, an excellent leader must share their professional insights and patterns with the team, fostering a unified way of thinking and communication within the team, thereby enhancing combat effectiveness.

Mr. Lu, VP of Digital China, graduated with a degree in microelectronics in 1999 and has been working in this field ever since. He joined Digital China in 2006, initially working in DIY parts sales. From 2009 to 2021, the sales volume of the microelectronics business he managed expanded a staggering 24 times. This exceptional growth can be attributed to his deep expertise and sensitivity developed over years of immersion in the microelectronics industry. Mr. Lu has a habit of chatting with industry friends every evening after work. His communication network includes suppliers, customers, salespeople and scholars. Early the next morning, he conducts his 'morning session,' organizing the information gathered the previous night to assess the market trends of the day, thereby guiding business decisions. Whether it is selecting partners, deciding the quantity of goods to distribute through various channels or setting the pricing for a specific IC, these are all within his scope of decision-making and consideration. His professional decisions are supported by his deep dedication to his field and his long-term commitment to information collection and comprehensive thinking.

The second level is the ability to lead a team, which requires strong interpersonal skills. The company prides itself on 'moving from victory to victory,' aiming to elevate every task and project to a higher level and ensuring that each transformation leads the entire company to a greater height. How can leaders guide the team to move from victory to victory? In addition to professional expertise and personal capability, leaders must also possess excellent interpersonal skills to build and maintain a strong team. That is essential for true leadership, as a leader must not only be capable of individual success but also proficient in team leadership, guiding everyone to collective victories. A leader's authority and momentum stem from the team's outstanding performance. A leader who frequently leads the team to failure will undoubtedly lack authority and potential energy. Even a leader who has achieved great things in their field and within the company must prove themselves in a new organization by leading the team to victories, thereby earning the team's trust and respect and building authority within the new team.

The current president of DCITS, Mr. Li, is the first talent we have brought in from a foreign enterprise. After joining the company, he led the team to achieve outstanding business results. His authority was established not because of his high academic qualifications or eloquence but because he genuinely managed to excel in handling major client businesses. Following the establishment of DCITS's fintech strategy, he faced new challenges, leading the growth and development of the company's fintech business. He did not shy away from these challenges; instead, he began learning financial knowledge anew and led the team to confront and overcome numerous difficulties required for strategic transformation. These included challenges in operational performance, team management and market value management – none of which were easy. He navigated these challenges steadily. Today, both the team and clients respect him, not because of his title as president but because he has become an industry expert and can consistently lead the team to victories.

Good interpersonal relationships also require leaders to be effective storytellers. Even if a leader cannot explain technical content as thoroughly as a technical expert, they can still convey the essence of the company by telling compelling stories based on their own experiences. Being able to narrate the company's story clearly and engagingly helps others understand and connect with the organization. If a leader cannot articulate their company's story and merely reads text from a PowerPoint presentation in a dry manner, it won't be easy to demonstrate leadership.

In addition to professional expertise and interpersonal skills, the third level requires strategic vision. If a company's leadership only focuses on immediate gains, it will not last long, and the organization will lack true leadership. When Digital China was founded, if we had only pursued profitable ventures, many people would have left long ago. Our goal is to use the science, technology and knowledge we possess to change China and the world, not just to make money. This broader vision is what allows the company to grow bigger.

On a smaller scale, strategic vision means recognizing trends in societal and technological development, understanding the gaps between societal needs and current supply, and identifying real business opportunities to keep the company thriving. On a larger scale, strategic vision involves choosing the best paths to fulfil the company's mission and vision. Leaders at different levels must have the ability to select these optimal paths. Without a method to achieve their ideals, leaders cannot establish potential energy.

In summary, a leader's momentum stems from the authority built through battles and challenges. That requires leaders to become experts in their professional fields, unite team members, foresee future trends and design paths to success. If leaders in certain departments lack authority, it is because they have not achieved these three critical aspects.

2. THE POWER OF BELIEF – VISION, MISSION, VALUES

In addition to being a role model, a leader must possess momentum and belief. Belief consists of the things we firmly believe in – our vision, mission and values. These shared beliefs can unite people, as everyone is brought together for a common vision and mission, not for any individual or specific project. Every organization must have such ideals and beliefs; otherwise, it cannot be called an organization.

I have great respect for Michael Yu,[23] a remarkable entrepreneur whose New Oriental grew from a dilapidated classroom outside Peking University to become an industry leader and pioneer in the capital markets. However, with the implementation of certain policies, the rapid growth of the education and training industry came to an abrupt halt, catching all institutions off guard.

Like other education and training institutions, New Oriental faced a crisis: the company's market value plummeted, subject training for compulsory education was shut down, tens of thousands of families were waiting for tuition refunds, and 60,000 employees were awaiting severance pay. Yet, New Oriental did not make headlines with negative news about parents demanding refunds or employees complaining about unpaid wages on social media. Why?

The reason is that Michael Yu refunded 20 billion RMB to all students and paid severance to employees. At an entrepreneur forum, he spoke about this with deep emotion: "Fortunately, New Oriental still had money. If we had no money, even if I had to sell everything I owned, I might have jumped off a building."

Not only did Michael Yu refund the tuition fees, but he also donated 80,000 sets of desks and chairs and other items to underprivileged rural schools.

That is the responsibility and spirit of an entrepreneur. When an era ends, some leave in disarray, while others depart with dignity and grace. Michael Yu managed to exit gracefully.

Of course, New Oriental's story did not end there. A year later, in the live-streaming sales sector, a company called Oriental Selection emerged as a dark horse. Oriental Selection was a new venture by New Oriental, and they succeeded.

Many people are curious about why Oriental Selection succeeded; the reason is because it is a company with belief, faith and camaraderie from top to bottom. Under the dual pressure of educational industry reform and the COVID-19 pandemic, this company's shared values and collective perseverance enabled it to emerge stronger.

In running our business today, we often encounter difficulties. Without a pursuit of belief, it is impossible to develop if we retreat at the first sign of trouble. If our employees simply jump ship because they think others are offering higher salaries, then the team's cohesion is in jeopardy. While competitive salaries are necessary to attract and retain talent, they should not be the sole bond between employees and the company. Therefore, while we do not require everyone to have the same level of commitment, we must have a core group of employees who have ideals and beliefs and are willing to share the company's ups and downs. Good compensation should reward excellent performance but should not be the only driving force.

A vision is essentially a forward-looking perspective that clarifies what kind of company we aim to become. As leaders of a company, we need to have foresight, the ability to stand high and see far, to foresee future changes and thus lead the team to go further. People often joke that if they could travel back 20 years, they would tell their past selves to buy property, knowing that the real estate industry has grown rapidly in the past two decades, yielding high returns on investment. Similarly, a company's strategy involves predicting future trends and being firmly committed to these predictions, willing to invest time, resources and energy.

However, fundamentally, a vision is a prediction about the future not yet visible to everyone. Enhancing one's insight, improving the accuracy of forecasts and getting everyone to believe in it are critical aspects of leadership. Digital China aims to be a leading partner of digital transformation that collaborates with our channels, customers and employees. 'Leading' means being ahead in concepts, technology and practice. Additionally, emphasizing 'partners' underlines the importance of an ecosystem.

As early as 1999, a professor at a business school said that entrepreneurs entering the 21st century were characterized by self-awareness and intuition. We remember Steve Jobs because he was a genius entrepreneur who embodied these traits. His unique grasp of the market, combined with his dedication and persistence in technological innovation, led Apple to achieve great success. From revamping Apple's notebook computers to inventing the iPod, and later the iPhone and the iPad, and launching the App Store and iCloud, Jobs built an excellent industrial chain and created a remarkable competitive edge for Apple. The key was his clear vision of the future direction of the entire information technology industry and his relentless pursuit of it. If he could not see the future and thought the same as everyone else, he would not be Steve Jobs, and there would be no Apple.

Having a vision also necessitates a sense of mission. What is a mission? Essentially, it is a question of social identity recognition. In our pursuit of that vision, what role do we play? What kind of social identity do we hope to embody? It is our mission. Why does Digital China aim to create a 'Digital China'? It is because China is undergoing a digital transformation, and we believe that building a 'Digital China' is something we can and should do. This identity enables us to gain social recognition. Once this identity is established, our entire team will have a stronger sense of mission. It is not just the leadership team but all our employees who should identify with this future-oriented mission.

The ancient Greek philosophers, who influenced the foundational principles of modern science, discovered something significant known as the first principle. Every matter has a fundamental proposition and assumption that cannot be defaulted or violated. In everything we do, we must reflect on our original intentions. Our vision and mission are our original intentions. Maintaining these intentions provides us with a guiding principle for our actions.

In a sense, a mission involves treating others' tasks as our own. Treating national goals as our own gives us potential energy. By doing what society needs, we attract societal resources to help us achieve these tasks. Previously, our IT product distribution and IT services, and now our fintech initiatives, align with what the country needs most in its digital transformation. By treating these tasks as our own, we achieve success smoothly. Personal profit lacks social value.

Once the mission is defined, evaluating subsequent business activities requires us to frequently ask ourselves how these activities relate to the company's mission. For Digital China, continuous transformation is driven by a commitment to the vision of 'Digital China' amid changing survival environments. Digital China aspires to engage in imaginative business ventures, not merely to achieve higher stock prices in the capital market but to urge ourselves to integrate closely with the significant development of the era and jointly promote societal progress. Digital China encourages employees to interact with customers not just with the mindset of selling products but also with the belief that they are fulfilling a mission.

Achieving a corporate mission requires both unwavering belief in our core principles and diligent adherence to our values. Values are the behavioral guidelines for handling various relationships. Though the term may seem abstract, values constantly influence every decision we make in our daily lives.

For instance, Chinese culture highly regards the values of loyalty, righteousness and integrity. Loyalty is fundamental. Without loyalty in an organization, if people 'bite the hand that feeds you,' they will be disrespected and lack leadership. Righteousness is related to our mission; the work we do should serve the greater good, not just short-term interests. What is integrity? We say, "Fulfil the entrusted tasks with utmost loyalty," meaning that we must honor our commitments at all costs.

If a person is unkind to their parents, how can others trust them in a partnership? A person's attitude toward friends and family might seem irrelevant to their professional life, but it reflects their behavior patterns. If someone is unfaithful to their parents and friends, how can you trust them to honor commitments in a business relationship? If you need to guard against them in every transaction, mutual trust in the company will erode, hindering its development. Therefore, values are not abstract concepts but concrete behavioral guidelines.

Digital China was one of the earliest to propose the values of responsibility, passion, innovation and sharing, which essentially promote a set of values defining the relationships between individuals within the organization and between individuals and the company. Digital China has always sought to enhance organizational leadership through the cultivation of these values. For example, how do we foster a culture that does not to be overly critical? A culture that, when faced with problems and failures, does not resort to complaints and finger-pointing? Digital China hopes that when difficulties and dangers arise, employees first think about taking responsibility, then reflect and summarize. Only when leaders and employees at all levels proactively take responsibility can we create an atmosphere that encourages innovation. In other words, Digital China aims to cultivate the spirit of standing back up where you fall, continuously summarizing experiences and lessons learned. The more difficult the times and the more problems that arise, the more leaders at all levels should step back, use dialectical thinking and innovation to discover new opportunities, and then apply effective methods to practice. When internal strategies do not work, external strategies should be considered. Only in this way can an innovative corporate culture be fostered.

Looking to the future, to make our organization more resilient, agile and strong, we have synthesized the common denominators of past experiences, current philosophies and future challenges to form new core values: champion customer success, create value, pursue excellence and foster shared growth. Achieving customers is the starting point for all decisions, creating value is the standard by which all work is measured, pursuing excellence is our approach to work and life, and being open and win-win is our vision and ultimate goal. These interconnected values drive everyone in the organization forward.

How to implement corporate values?

First, it starts with management. As a Chinese historical work written in the sixth century about a utopian model of ideal government, *Zhenguan Zhengyao* (*The Essentials of Governance of the Zhenguan Reign*) states, "One cannot be upright oneself and have a crooked shadow, nor govern well from the top and have chaos below." The senior management team of a company plays a direct role in demonstrating the implementation of corporate values. If managers at all levels consciously practice these values and create a strong corporate culture, it can have a subtle influence on employees, leading them from recognition to imitation and finally to conscious action. Therefore, a company's momentum is reflected in whether its management embodies the advocated values. From another perspective, if every manager exudes corporate values, they will have the power to lead and achieve great things.

Second, implementing corporate values requires focusing on habit formation. Corporate values are not just slogans on the wall; they must be internalized and reflected in actions. It means that practising corporate values is not a one-time effort but a process of gradual accumulation and subtle influence, forming habits in every action of all members. Therefore, the company must emphasize the construction of concepts and the formation of habits in its management process. If concepts are only written on paper and not integrated into daily operations and management, they cannot be effective. Through cultivating daily behaviors, corporate values can silently and imperceptibly influence organizational members, leading them to accept and practice these values sincerely.

Finally, institutional guarantees must be established to implement corporate values. The formation and practice of corporate values is a long and complex process that requires the support of systems and processes to be truly realized. Specifically, a clear system of rewards and penalties must be established to encourage behaviors that practise corporate values and punish those who violate them. That ensures the authority of corporate values and gradually internalizes them within the company and its members' behaviors, creating consistency in corporate actions. It, in turn, enhances the company's core competitiveness and promotes long-term development.

3. THE POWER OF GROWTH – UNDERSTAND, PRACTISE, RE-UNDERSTAND AND RE-PRACTISE

If we compare knowledge to a vast, chaotic ocean and our understanding of a sphere floating within it, the more we learn, the larger the sphere becomes. Correspondingly, we become increasingly aware of our ignorance.

Aristotle proposed the geocentric model, believing that the Earth was the centre of the universe. Nicolaus Copernicus, before his death, proposed the heliocentric model. Today, we understand that even the sun is not the centre of the universe. Isaac Newton defined classical mechanics, laying the foundation for the entire industrial revolution. However, Albert Einstein discovered that classical mechanics was just a special case of his theory of relativity in slow-moving conditions because classical mechanics assumes that speed is relative. Albert Einstein introduced the concept of relativity to explain the constant speed of light.

In 2016, the launch of the Micius Satellite for Quantum Science Experiments marked China's leading position in the field of quantum communication. The principle used in quantum communication – quantum entanglement – was once dismissed by Albert Einstein. Quantum entanglement is like a telepathic connection between twins; no matter how far apart two quantum particles are, their states remain correlated. Albert Einstein found this unbelievable. However, today, we can prove that this phenomenon objectively exists, demonstrating that even great scientists have their cognitive limitations.

From classical mechanics to quantum mechanics, there has been a monumental shift in human understanding of the microscopic world. Following this, Stephen William Hawking applied many methodologies, from quantum mechanics to the entire universe. Consequently, dark matter and dark energy, which are unobservable to humans, were discovered. In the theory of relativity, the universe's position is relatively static. However, the theory of the Big Bang tells us that the universe is constantly expanding.

Looking back, from Michael Faraday's discovery of the electromagnetic field in 1831 to James Clerk Maxwell's establishment of a complete electromagnetic theory, from the development of the telegraph in Great Britain and the United States in the 1830s to Alexander Graham Bell's invention of the telephone in 1876, from John Ambrose Fleming's invention of the first electron tube to the birth of the first computer, ENIAC, in 1946, and then to Tim Berners-Lee's proposal of the World Wide Web in 1989; from the concepts of cloud computing introduced by Amazon and Google 20 years ago to the explosion of AI, and now to the metaverse. In just over 100 years, human life has undergone tremendous changes. We have become amphibians, living in both the physical and virtual worlds.

Cognitive limitations are inherent, and we emphasize the vision of breaking through these self-imposed boundaries continually. An individual's understanding determines their actions. From a company's perspective, its perception of the world will decide its destiny, and its view of society and the world will determine its innovation high ground.

The greatest challenge in business management is the impact of new circumstances on our concepts, thinking methods and culture. Can the organization clearly see the future in the face of new situations and environments amid the enormous uncertainties of the future? Or will it remain immersed in the joy of past success? When new business conflicts with traditional business, how should we view and understand new technologies, new thinking and new organizational methods?

Things also develop beyond people's expectations. If we do not fundamentally transform our thinking and break through our cognitive limitations, we will be doomed to fail. It is a basic survival rule for businesses. When facing such opportunities and challenges, there is only one way out – to create a blue ocean and embark on a path of value innovation and growth. To build a bigger and more brilliant enterprise, one must go through a process of constant self-denial, achieving success through continuous change and adjustment.

To break through cognitive limitations, one must continuously enhance their learning ability.

What is learning? A baby learns to speak without obstacles, like a parrot mimicking sounds. In elementary school, learning is natural. Learning continues through college and into early career stages, where learning and asking questions are normal and not shameful. However, after achieving success, learning seems to become very difficult. People prefer to enjoy their success rather than learn from others.

Learning is not just reading books, attending classes or listening to lectures – these are superficial. The most important aspects are self-reflection, reading, experiencing, imagining, and innovative, systematic thinking – these are fundamental. The learning process is one of understanding, practising, re-understanding and re-practising. The purpose of learning is to grasp the truth and the laws of world change. Mastering these laws allows one to work with ease, while not mastering them leads to constant obstacles.

In the process of running a business, no task can be perfected from the outset; it will inevitably require continuous iteration and refinement. All our summarized experiences come from practice and are applied back into practice. In our business operations, each customer has unique characteristics. We should not assume that the next customer will be served in the same way as the previous one.

Each customer is different, and we must identify both the commonalities and specificities. While commonalities can be applied to the next customer, specificities cannot.

An organization should become a learning organization, fostering a nonbureaucratic atmosphere. Every individual within the organization should learn. From whom should we learn? Not only should we learn from theoretical sources, superiors and knowledgeable individuals, but we also need to learn from our employees, competitors and everyone we encounter. Engaging with each person can yield valuable knowledge. Particularly, learning from their precious practical experiences is invaluable. If we can absorb, digest and transform these into personal experiences to guide practical work, it becomes even more commendable.

The senior management team teaches the youth cadre training courses at Digital China. They summarize their excellent practical experiences into methodologies and pass them on to the trainees. After the courses, everyone applies these methodologies in practice, creating case studies that, in turn, enrich the original methods. That is also a process of understanding, practising, re-understanding and re-practising. This talent development system, from best practices to methodologies, is then refined and promoted, gradually forming a unified organizational language that serves the company's development.

Cognition is limited, while the world is infinite. Even the most fundamental understanding can be challenged and overturned. However, we cannot let the possibility of being proven wrong stop us from pursuing knowledge. Having this mindset and habit enables continuous progress. For an organization, forward-thinking cognition prompts us to continually embrace new changes, helping us seize new business opportunities and release accumulated advantages in new circumstances. Forward-thinking cognition is precisely the starting point for Digital China's continuous transformation.

4. THE POWER OF INSIGHT – UNDERSTAND PATTERNS

The final aspect of increasing momentum is understanding patterns. To transcend oneself, it is not enough to set visions and goals; one must also grasp the patterns of development. Without understanding these patterns, achieving our goals becomes very difficult or even impossible. In the previous section, we discussed the importance of learning and growth. The purpose of learning is to grasp the truth and understand the patterns of change in the world.

When discussing understanding patterns, there are at least two dimensions to consider. One is how the economic and social environments are changing; we need to discern societal evolution patterns and government policy directions, as these form the macro-environment in which we survive. The other is sensing future trends in science and technology, particularly how IT technology will drive transformations, as this is our foundation. Working in the computer industry, we must have an understanding of the patterns in computer development. This ability to understand patterns is essential for strategic planning.

In the field of information technology, particularly data, disruptive technologies are certain to emerge in the future. In 2015, I had a whimsical thought: Humanity has undergone revolutions in the physical world and the data world and will eventually undergo a revolution in the life world, which might conclude the course of history. Why? We all know that Albert Einstein proposed $E=mc^2$, clarifying the relationship between mass and energy, thus explaining the physical world. From the advent of computers to now, we have been exchanging information through something without mass, creating a virtual world. The revolution in the world of life pertains to genes, which combine mass and information and then replicate. If the genetic revolution enables everyone to live for 300 years, the Earth might not be able to accommodate the population.

Later, based on practical experience, I kept pondering: What exactly is the digital revolution? It may involve three changes.

The first change is the evolution of IT technology.

Over the past few decades, we've observed that, following Moore's Law, computing power has been rapidly increasing. This growth in computing power has triggered a series of changes. Chips are used not only in computers but also in mobile phones, today's televisions, razors and rice cookers, all of which contain CPUs. By leveraging computing methods, we can enhance these products with better interactions and smarter functionalities. The mass production of computing power has reduced production and R&D costs, leading to the widespread availability of computing power. This widespread availability has driven consumer demand which, in turn, has reinvested into industry R&D. The externalities brought by the IT industry have a universally beneficial impact on society.

The architecture of computers is also evolving. Take IBM, for example. It started with mainstream architecture, moved to network architecture, then to internet architecture, and now to cloud architecture. The current cloud architecture has brought a series of changes to the digital world. Years ago, I discussed with a computer industry expert whether, after CPUs, operating systems and database middleware, there would be an application architecture or infrastructure. At that time, the concept of the cloud did not exist, and the path of architectural evolution was unclear. We thought there should be a breakthrough in this area. Although we conceived the idea then, we didn't pursue innovation in that direction, which I regret. Today, the PaaS layer of the cloud serves as an infrastructure for applications. The continuous evolution of architecture provides stronger support for applications similar to container technology.

In the transportation field, what events led to the revolutionary changes we see today? Many might think it was the engine or some new means of transportation. However, it wasn't these high-tech advancements but the advent of the container that truly broke through the interaction bottlenecks between rail, ship and air transport. Without containers, imagine what our transportation would look like today and what the efficiency of logistics would be. Our current use of containers is like those in the transportation industry – they may not seem highly technical, but they are incredibly practical. When we use Application

Programming Interfaces (APIs) to place data into containers, it enables seamless communication of information between different clouds, making data and services flow smoothly and significantly increasing the efficiency of computing services. Therefore, I believe APIs are very important, and this technology is still evolving. How it will develop is something worth paying attention to.

This macro-level understanding is very important. Only by mastering the development patterns of the industry can we avoid spending time heading in the wrong direction. Throughout the development cycle of the entire enterprise, we must focus on both the present and the future, act according to the trends, follow objective laws and seek development paths. If we grasp these patterns, we will know what to do.

The second change is the revolution in cognitive science. Big data is a crucial concept; fundamentally, it represents a revolution in cognitive science. Historically, modern science became possible only with Newton's first law, allowing us to quantify and explain physical phenomena using data methods. After a series of developments and changes, information enterprises emerged. However, information itself is not new; it has existed alongside humans, such as our language. Language and writing are forms of information expression. Before digitization and the internet, information was isolated and dispersed, unable to form a truly interconnected virtual world. With the advent of information science, the virtual world emerged. Functions facilitated scientific computation, and later, databases enabled commercial computation. Further on, social computation involves modelling various entities in society based on our understanding of them. We model pigs, grass, factories and logistics – this is digital twin technology, which is our objective. In essence, big data is cognitive science. What should we do in this field? That is something we need to consider.

When we examine the current era, we often mention the leap from the physical world to the virtual world. We use atoms to represent the physical world and bits to represent the virtual world. So, what are the laws of atoms? What are the laws of bits? From networking to the cloud, from big data to artificial intelligence, what are the underlying patterns? How do these patterns change?

Traditionally, information technology involves the collection, storage, computation and analysis of information, followed by profiling and application based on these processes. These steps cycle repeatedly. In the internet era, IT infrastructure was built to support these functions, considering constraints like computing power and bandwidth. During the early internet days, when connections were made via telephone lines, the core issue was bandwidth expansion. Cisco brought routers, and IP access methods significantly changed bandwidth capabilities. Cellular networks, fibre optics and other technologies enabled the transition of transmitted content from audio to video, from text to images, and then to high-definition video. The rise of artificial intelligence is a natural consequence of advancements in semiconductors, communications and computer technology. Without high-speed computing chips from the semiconductor field, high-bandwidth communication equipment from the communication field and big data support from industry applications, artificial intelligence would not be possible.

What's next? It is cloud-native and digital-native. Humanity is no longer satisfied with merely collecting and transmitting services to serve the physical world. Instead, a new world will be reconstructed in the digital realm. New virtual entities will be created in the virtual world as containers for new meanings, accommodating content that cannot be realized in the physical world.

The third change is the scenarios. Any technology needs an application scenario to be meaningful; it must be combined with a business or an application, leading to integrated innovation. Where does innovation occur? It happens in specific scenarios. For example, a car is essentially a combination of a means of transportation and an engine. It is the application of engine technology and a series of auxiliary technologies in the transportation scenario. Alipay and WeChat Pay are examples of mobile internet technology applied in the payment scenario. Our innovation should focus on how to use new technologies to combine and enhance current business operations.

Developing and utilizing scenarios requires not only an understanding of objective laws but also imagination. Before James Watt invented the steam engine, steam was just a common, unnoticed phenomenon. Gunpowder was used for religious rituals before being utilized in firearms. Consider a bowl of rice: a homemaker can cook a bowl of rice worth one RMB, which is its most basic value; a worker can make a few rice dumplings, earning two to three RMB; a factory owner can brew a bottle of Baijiu (Chinese liquor) worth 20 RMB; and an entrepreneur can further refine and mass-produce Baijiu, adding cultural characteristics to increase its value significantly.

Dramatic scenarios are an embodiment of imagination. William Shakespeare is considered great because he created dozens of plays that defined the elements and theoretical framework of drama, using dramatic language to perfectly present scenes. With these elements, works can be continually reproduced. Isaac Newton's contribution lies in his clear definition of the research paradigm for classical mechanics, laying the foundation for classical physics. Today, we still use the principles and concepts defined by Isaac Newton. It can be said that most of our research still operates within the 'scientific scenario' defined by Isaac Newton.

So, how do we imagine and define application scenarios? We are not prophets, and many things cannot be predicted, but the major trends and patterns are traceable. Why did the ancients say, "Reading ten thousand books is not as good as travelling ten thousand miles"? It means that continuous practice is necessary. Through practice, we provide feedback to theory – whether positive or negative – constantly enriching our understanding and broadening our thinking.

ACHIEVE CONSENSUS THROUGH EFFECTIVE COMMUNICATION

In the previous section, we discussed that a significant part of momentum comes from ideals and views of the future. Leaders who define their vision and strategy based on their judgements gain a certain amount of momentum. However, if these ideas cannot influence others, they cannot build a successful team. A team with leadership and excellence maintains consistency in values, strategic direction and even key operational steps. Such an organization is invincible.

Therefore, we emphasize that the second element of leadership is communication. Leaders must use various communication methods to disseminate these beliefs, goals and proven ways of doing things throughout the company. It ensures that everyone can reach a consensus and create resonance within the company and even within the industry. Only by achieving such consensus can an organization build momentum, effectively implement strategies and not be limited to individual foresight.

The fundamental purpose of communication is to enhance consensus. A team is made up of individuals, and if there is no unity, even the greatest individual strength cannot create team synergy. As the saying goes, "When people are united, they can move Mount Tai." When an organization cannot gather consensus on major directions, its power cannot be effectively exerted. Achieving consensus is essentially the mutual dissemination and influence of thoughts and ideas; it is a process. A concept introduced into the organization is like a pebble thrown into the water, causing ripples that spread outward.

Throw enough pebbles, and the ripples will interact – overlapping or cancelling each other – creating a dynamic pattern of resonance.

Truth can be spread, and so can rumors. Without intervention, information within an organization will continually increase entropy, tending toward disorder. Therefore, we focus on the formal and positive transmission of information within the organization, which differs from casual, unstructured conversations; it is a purposeful and structured form of communication. The promotion of weekly work reports within the organization is aimed at cascading key company tasks down through structured, written communication, ultimately creating company-wide consensus.

We must also recognize that communication extends beyond internal communication to external communication. To build a core competency of customer-centricity, we place high demands on key account managers for their communication skills. They cannot merely focus on their existing business – selling only software if they do software, only hardware if the managers do hardware, or only services if they do services. Instead, they need to understand all the company's products. Many things can be communicated to customers through account managers, so they need to have a comprehensive understanding of the company's history, structure and various aspects.

In the process of advancing our strategy, everyone in the company is both a sower and a promoter. We need to sow the seeds of Digital China's vision of 'Digital China' across the country, sharing our story with clients, friends, classmates and colleagues. Rather than engaging in idle chit-chat, it's more productive to talk about our company – this is how we sow seeds everywhere.

During this process, it might happen that a friend's child, who graduated from a prestigious university like Stanford, hears good things about Digital China and decides to join us, adding a high-level talent to the company. Or someone might have learned about our successful business and decides to buy our stock, gradually expanding the company's influence.

When everyone in the company promotes it, making others feel that we are indeed a good company, we can attract more talented people and investments.

If all the 20,000 employees of our company care about it in this way, telling their friends or various community members a good story about our company, our influence will grow significantly. That is the work we need to do to strengthen the team's consistency and reach a consensus.

Consensus is necessary, but achieving it is challenging. In practical work, there are often five levels of reasons why consensus cannot be reached:

First, limited cognition. Different business units have varying customer types, business models, operational rhythms, risk types and strategies for dealing with those risks. These diverse perspectives can lead to mutual misunderstandings. To overcome cognitive limitations, business leaders should actively listen, ask questions and think critically. The company should also organize both formal and informal communications at various levels to promote mutual understanding.

Second, conflicting interests. Due to differing short-term and long-term interests, some individuals might 'pretend to sleep.' Even if they know which decisions are correct, they may not act on them or acknowledge them because it affects their interests. This type of conflict often arises because people view situations as zero-sum games, inevitably leading to a win-lose struggle. In resolving such obstacles, it is essential to adopt a higher perspective and create win-win scenarios.

Third, information loss in transmission. Information loss is inevitable during the transmission process. To minimize this loss, we need to reduce it as much as possible or add amplifiers in the middle. Acting as amplifiers requires leveraging the level of belief. A team can achieve success not just because of an exceptional leader but because the team shares a common faith and consensus. They act as amplifiers, continually magnifying the strategic guidelines agreed upon by the leadership team across different contexts and fields, effectively countering the loss in transmission.

Fourth, outsider mentality. Some colleagues speak from an insider's perspective, raising questions, while others take an outsider's stance, saying, "How is your company doing?" But aren't they part of the company, too? If the company encounters problems, it affects everyone. The outsider mentality includes not only the attitude toward the company but also toward different business units. For example, someone involved in traditional business might think that new strategic business has nothing to do with them and only cares about their area. This phenomenon is difficult to avoid, as there will always be people who feel it's not their concern. However, with an outsider mentality, it's impossible to reach a consensus.

Fifth, fear of conflict. When collaborating, differing opinions can lead to disputes. Although everyone rationally understands that issues should be discussed factually, in practice, people often tend to avoid confrontation. Many individuals inherently dislike conflicts, preferring to prevent creating disputes and offending others. However, a mature organization should have appropriate ways to bring conflicts and disagreements into the open, addressing and resolving them positively. Fear of conflicts prevents genuine problem-solving.

We will discuss solutions for each of the five major obstacles mentioned above.

1. THE COMPLEXITY OF BUSINESS: CHALLENGES TO CONSENSUS

Our business is highly complex. Different business units have varying operational cycles, success factors and key areas of focus. This complexity leads to diverse ways of thinking. These differing perspectives can make it challenging for the team to reach a consensus when needed.

Initially, Digital China focused on distribution, a business with a 30-day cycle, making it easy to see operational results. Then, we moved into Value-Added Distribution (VAD), which has a cycle of about 60 days. Later, we ventured into integration, extending the cycle to 180 days, where we could see the business outcomes after six months. In the service and software sectors, however, the operational cycles may span over a year. How do we account for this? As the business complexity and difficulty increase, the time cycles for calculating investment returns get longer and more challenging.

Currently, most of our service business is still product-based, which is relatively simple. A genuine service business is more akin to performing surgery. Imagine a patient on the operating table, anaesthetized, ready for tumor removal. Upon opening the abdominal cavity, the tumor is found to have spread. How do we adjust the surgical plan? How do we communicate with the patient and their family? After surgery, how do we change the postoperative recovery plan? The challenges we face in the service business are like this example. The complexity of calculating investment returns in this context is entirely different from that in distribution or integration.

Now we have taken a step further by developing our products, which is further increasing complexity. It adds a supply chain management dimension, extending the time cycle further. It lengthens the return-on-investment period, making it harder to calculate returns accurately.

Our cloud business introduces an entirely different business model, with even longer intervals between investment and returns than our proprietary products. It brings us to the dilemma of balancing short-term and long-term interests. Short-term benefits are easier to understand, but long-term benefits imply that today's investments might take one, two or even three years to yield returns. Do we have the determination to pursue this? That involves judgement and the consensus that follows.

Currently, DCITS focuses on a fintech strategy, facing the trade-off between highly profitable but less strategically aligned mature businesses and strategic fintech initiatives. Will our fintech business achieve the set goals in the next three years? That is a critical question. If we allocate all resources in one direction and fail to meet the targets after three years, what will we do? These strategic consensus issues need discussion and increased alignment.

Why pursue fintech 2.0? It opens up a strategic vision. Our future fintech business will differ from the past, integrating the concept of data cloud integration and opening a longer-term perspective. Once our long-term goals are established, short-term interest considerations will diminish.

As business managers, we must contemplate whether to always focus on short-cycle business or to transform the company's organizational value, making our business more technologically advanced and creating greater value for society. If we merely stick to our old business models, we won't be able to increase our societal contributions, and both the company's and individuals' returns will be affected. The relationship between the internal sales team and the company will become a static game, leading to organizational management issues.

Therefore, we need to drive growth from our business and push the organization toward higher value directions. Only when the expected societal value of our business is high can we attract more outstanding talent. Better value outcomes will lead to higher market value, providing us with more funds to invest in long-term initiatives and allowing our employees to share in better value returns. Why did Amazon's market value continue to rise despite consecutive quarterly losses? Its investment in technology and its innovation leads to the industry's progress. When we talk about leadership, we're not just referring to individual leadership within the organization but also to the company's role as an industry leader, taking on social responsibilities and gaining societal respect. These ideas are interconnected.

Of course, facing the dilemma of balancing long-term and short-term goals can be challenging, and it's normal to be unclear at times, often resulting in a 'foot in both camps' situation, seeking both long-term and short-term benefits. That is a common challenge for most companies, except for startups, which always have a clear goal – either they succeed and grow, or they fail. It is a process of continuous adjustment and clarity. Therefore, maintaining a long-lasting enterprise and becoming a century-old company is not easy.

To increase value, we must continuously expand the input-output ratio of our products and services, create products and services with increasing marginal benefits, and calculate the total returns over long cycles. For example, in the software business, the larger the customer base, the lower the marginal cost. Take operating system software as an example: if a company invests 1 billion RMB in development but only has one customer, that customer's cost is 1 billion RMB. However, if there are 100 million customers, the cost is divided into 10 RMB per customer. Any amount charged over 10 RMB per customer becomes profit. That is the advantage of low-cost, replicable products. Traditional solutions, with a limited customer base, cannot cover high development costs.

Digital China's cloud business follows a similar logic. Although we don't sell standardized, low-cost, replicable products, we can repeatedly sell to the same customer, which is also an accumulative process. If we have one million customers, each paying us 1 RMB, we earn 1 million RMB, allowing us to invest 1 million RMB to develop a product. If each customer pays 10 RMB, we can invest 10 million RMB; if each pays 100 RMB, we can invest 100 million RMB. The product developed with a 100 million RMB investment will naturally be different from one developed with 1 million RMB. Therefore, predicting the future size of the customer base is crucial in business planning.

Why do we need to transform? Because we must shift from short cycles to long cycles, focusing on more valuable long-term endeavors, which is our driving force. Currently, most of our company leaders come from distribution and integration backgrounds, which ensures short-term benefits but also creates conflicts between short-term and long-term business goals. It isn't easy to logically persuade everyone to forgo today's benefits for long-term gains, as our future predictions are probabilistic, unlike the certainty of short-term benefits. We live in uncertain times, and while it's challenging, we must accept uncertainty as the norm.

Returning to our theme, a core difficulty in achieving consensus is pursuing a goal in an ever-changing, uncertain environment. If everything were certain, achieving business goals would be straightforward because everyone would know the direction to take. However, determining goals amid uncertainty is a significant challenge. This evolving environment and business growth process create real difficulties in achieving consensus. Recognizing difficulties doesn't guarantee solutions, but acknowledging them is the first step – from 'not knowing what we don't know' to 'knowing what we don't know,' enabling us to address them.

Addressing consensus difficulties caused by cognitive challenges begins with acknowledging 'knowing what we don't know.' We must dare to ask probing questions and persist until we understand. If something isn't clear, it may not be due to our lack of ability but rather the explanation's clarity. By continuously asking questions, we can understand different business models and expand our cognitive scope. Organizationally, to enhance mutual understanding among departments and business units, we can establish informal communication channels alongside formal ones, promoting mutual understanding within the organization.

2. CREATION OF A WIN-WIN SITUATION FROM A HIGHER PERSPECTIVE

Often, the inability to reach consensus stems from differing interests among parties. In corporate management, these inconsistencies manifest as various pressures, such as market competition, shareholder pressure, employee pressure and customer pressure.

There is the pressure from market competition, which is the most direct pressure. Without market competition, we could gradually achieve our strategic goals. However, when competition arises, it can disrupt existing mechanisms and rhythms. Whether in market marketing, mergers and acquisitions, or talent competition, the pressure from competitors is the most immediate. On one hand, we face numerous competitors with business models similar to ours, leading to confrontations. In such cases, competition is prevalent, though there is also the possibility of cooperation to capture more market share. On the other hand, the emergence of new technologies and business models brings unexpected potential competitors, often disruptive, causing greater pressure.

There is pressure from shareholders. Shareholders aim to maximize their investment value. While management undertakes various activities for the company's long-term development, shareholders' investments are cyclical. Balancing long-term and short-term interests to show returns to shareholders becomes a crucial management task. Many performance indicators might be the results of shareholder pressure. As a publicly listed company, we must pay attention to the capital market's perception of us. Market competition has significant asymmetry; others might see only limited data and performance, judging the company's situation from these alone. This situation requires us to excel in investor relations and comply with shareholder constraints, which often conflict with the internal team's ideas.

There is pressure from employees. Every employee hopes to maximize their benefits and value in the quickest way possible. How can these individual goals be aligned with the overall objectives of the company? It is mainly reflected in the systems and management methods, especially in how to genuinely guide and direct everyone in terms of thoughts and actions to face conflicts and challenges together. For example, balancing employees' demands for growth, income and recognition is crucial.

There is pressure from customers. If we only engage in distribution, the pressure from customers is not deeply felt. However, as we increasingly face customers directly and enhance our service efforts, the pressure intensifies. Compared to distribution, when providing solutions and services to major clients, the pressure experienced is significantly greater.

In fact, many conflicts cannot be effectively resolved at the same level and instead evolve into zero-sum games. Only by viewing problems from a higher perspective can we create win-win situations. Leadership, in the face of real pressures, is reflected in the ability to look at issues from a broader viewpoint and use wisdom and effective methods to create win-win or even multi-win scenarios. Whether dealing with customers, investors or employees, it's not a simple equation of 1+1=2; it is about how to make each '1' generate greater effects that benefit all parties involved. From international relations to interpersonal interactions, collaborations that benefit only one side are unsustainable. If a win-win situation cannot be created, why would others be motivated to follow?

For this reason, Digital China continuously innovates its cooperation models, evolving from 'four wins' to 'total aggregation.'

As early as 1998, when it was still called Lenovo Technology, Digital China proposed a four-win cooperation strategy, emphasizing mutual growth with suppliers, channel partners and users. For channel partners, Digital China promised, "We will ensure our channel partners make money; only their success in the market guarantees our success." Many small and medium-sized companies focused on distribution became beneficiaries of Digital China's commitment to its channel partners, growing and prospering alongside Digital China's business development.

After the spin-off and listing of Digital China, the distribution business began a new phase of transformation and upgrading. The company introduced the total aggregation cooperation model centred around channel partners. This model provides new momentum for channels through independent controllable products and cloud services. By building a digital marketing system, the company creates a comprehensive opportunity management system to enhance channel value. Additionally, a digital middle platform improves customer experience and reduces operational costs, thereby increasing channel efficiency. The company also opens up financing, human resources, risk management, and one-stop procurement capabilities and resources to partners, helping them solve problems. By reconstructing the cooperation model across products, services, branding and capital, Digital China fully supports its partners' digital transformation and brings innovation to the transformation of the distribution business model.

In our relationship with customers, we emphasize not just making money but achieving a win-win situation. It requires us to uphold a customer-centric mindset consistently. We must truly consider issues from the customer's perspective, identify their needs and then integrate our resources to serve them. During this service process, we may also spark new ideas and opportunities for further collaboration.

A classic example of a win-win relationship is the collaboration between DCITS and Bank B.

Bank B is a significant strategic partner for DCITS. Since 2008, the two companies have grown and developed together.

As a fintech service provider, DCITS offers Bank B a leading technology architecture based on cloud-native and microservices. They provide one-stop digital technology solutions in areas such as channels, customer acquisition, operations management and business development, deeply exploring the value of data assets to help the bank reduce costs and increase efficiency. The two companies also collaborate to explore innovative models in products, services, organization, processes and management mechanisms, expanding into scenario finance and ecosystem interconnection, effectively serving Bank B's development vision and practising DCITS's partner value.

When distributed technology first emerged in the financial industry, Bank B launched the Networked Construction Project of a Payment Clearing Platform, marking a positive attempt between the two parties. DCITS utilized a scalable, high-availability, high-performance, low-cost distributed technology system to meet the bank's requirements for large data volumes and high concurrency, laying the foundation for deeper future cooperation in distributed technology.

As their cooperation deepened, the two parties jointly explored innovative financial services. They developed online financing products to meet the short, frequent and urgent financing needs of SMEs, helping them secure online loan applications and disbursements. Based on this, Bank B also introduced a richer array of financial services, further enhancing its ability to serve the real economy and expand into the internet blue ocean.

The technological transformation in the digital age has brought new business models and developments. By staying at the forefront of fintech development, Bank B and DCITS's seamless cooperation has become a model of mutual growth and win-win cooperation between financial institutions and technology companies.

The relationship between the company and its employees is also a win-win situation. The company relies on its employees to achieve its overall strategic goals. In contrast, employees depend on the company to provide a platform for growth and development to realize their personal life goals. What attracts talent? What unites everyone's efforts? It is growing together with the company, which is the starting point for our human resource system design. Outstanding talents, when planning their career development, do not prioritize short-term salaries but rather seek a platform that mutually benefits their future career development, allowing for shared growth and shared rewards.

Within the company, we emphasize win-win scenarios, especially in the collaboration between various business units. For example, there is a natural cooperative relationship between distribution and supply chain businesses. Not only is distribution the largest customer of the supply chain business, but the expansion of supply chain services in repair and e-commerce also creates incremental business opportunities for distribution. Additionally, there are synergies between all business units and financial services. We can boldly apply Digital China's accumulated resources and capabilities in the IT field to financial services, using innovative financial scenarios to drive business innovation. If we can fully leverage the synergies between our business groups, we can break through conventional growth methods and create a unique, differentiated competitive advantage for Digital China.

From a team management perspective, we must create win-win situations. From the overall strategic level of the group, win-win is also the starting point for all of Digital China's actions. Digital China has grown alongside international companies like HP and Cisco in China. We have witnessed the winning strategies of global companies – the win-win strategy – and experienced the development momentum brought by mutual benefit and shared prosperity. Today, the concept of win-win remains unchanged, but Digital China's role is evolving from a learner to a transmitter, leading domestic enterprises in co-creating businesses and growing together, continuing to advance boldly along the path of mutual benefit.

3. REDUCTION OF 'SETTER' AND AVOIDANCE OF PARKINSON'S LAW TO UNIFY THOUGHT

In internal communication and information dissemination within an organization, it is crucial to prevent the problem of 'setter.' In volleyball, the setter is a player responsible for organizing the attack by making the second pass after receiving the ball from the opponent. On the volleyball court, the setter is one of the key organizers of the offence and tactics. They must possess not only skilled passing techniques but also the ability to adapt quickly, unite teammates and leverage the strengths of the entire team to organize the attack. Typically, each team has one or two setters who need to be resilient and calm, have a broad vision, have strong tactical awareness and be determined to execute strategic plans.

However, in a company, it is crucial to minimize the presence of middlemen. These middlemen in a company are those who, when faced with pending matters submitted by business departments, fail to fulfil their specialized advisory roles appropriately. Instead, they organize and pass on the information, ultimately causing delays in decision-making at the executive level due to inadequate information. Worse still, if these middlemen do not perform their transmission duties properly or act with selfish motives, it can lead to information distortion during the transmission process, resulting in misunderstandings between business departments and top management.

This phenomenon of information distortion is also known as 'information filtering.' Information filtering is a concept in organizational behavior that refers to the intentional manipulation of information by the sender to improve the receiver's perception of the information. If a manager only tells their superiors what the superior wants to hear, they are filtering information. Therefore, if the internal environment of the company is unhealthy and opposed to bad news, subordinates may only report positive news to please their superiors, leading to distorted upward communication and affecting transmission effectiveness. Thus, it is necessary to encourage all employees to think boldly and express their thoughts, create opportunities for communication and even establish corresponding reward mechanisms.

Another significant issue in organizational operations is Parkinson's Law, also known as Bureaucracy Disease, which exacerbates the middlemen phenomenon in companies. Parkinson's Law refers to a mediocre leader who hires two even more mediocre assistants to share his work while he remains in a high position issuing commands. By hiring less competent assistants, he ensures his authority is not threatened. However, because the assistants are incompetent, they, in turn, hire even less competent subordinates, thus creating a bloated organization with people shirking responsibilities, engaging in power struggles and operating inefficiently. This phenomenon is common in large enterprises, where a leader's secretary may have their secretary, and even that secretary might have a secretary. Many of these secretaries become middlemen. Parkinson's Law leads to an increase in middlemen, resulting in decreased efficiency in the information transmission process itself.

How can we avoid Parkinson's Law and reduce the phenomenon of middlemen?

First, after clarifying the strategic path, it is essential to define the timeline and key milestones clearly. This approach improves internal communication efficiency and minimizes the need for middlemen to the greatest extent possible.

When discussing corporate management, some people often think that goals and strategies have little to do with employees' work. However, this is not the case. For a company to effectively implement its goals and strategy and focus its resources on achieving tasks, everyone must be mobilized. If there is top-down agreement on the strategic path and milestones, the need for middlemen is fundamentally reduced.

Digital China's distribution business has been managed using a divisional system for many years, which is essentially a contracting system. The general managers of the divisions, as mid-level managers, become foremen whose primary responsibility is to ensure the achievement of sales and profit targets. This model aligns with China's traditional culture of 'farmers owning their fields,' and it effectively inspires a sense of responsibility among mid-level managers, cultivating a group of excellent divisional general managers. These managers not only ensure the achievement of sales tasks but also become undisputed sales experts in their respective fields.

However, under this model, some divisional general managers may prioritize the interests of their divisions over the interests of the company. When it comes to the company's annual strategic transformation tasks, they may only pay lip service without actual implementation, failing to allocate their time truly and their team's time toward strategic priority tasks. In terms of strategic transmission, these divisional general managers become middlemen, making it difficult for the company's strategic transformation efforts to penetrate the grassroots level.

In fact, establishing strategic thinking at the level of divisional general managers is highly significant. For these mid-level managers considering long-term career development, it is particularly important to break away from the middlemen mentality and actively understand the company's strategy. Only in this way can they proactively overcome the constraints of the original contracting system and achieve breakthroughs in their business. Take, for example, a division responsible for selling Product X.

1. Due to the strong service demands of Product X's customers, the division has strong customer service capabilities. Therefore, in addition to distributing products, it can also extend into independent, paid service businesses.
2. Furthermore, by leveraging its service capabilities, the division can establish industry solutions centred around X-type products, integrating a series of products serving that industry to provide better products and services to customers.

These approaches can lead to further business growth. However, if constrained by the contracting system and lacking an understanding of strategy, they often merely meet the annual operational figures, limiting their growth.

Many companies fail to escape Parkinson's Law due to a lack of effective time management methods aimed at strategic goals. This results in a significant waste of time and human resources, let alone execution capability. If detailed milestones are set for each day, week, month, quarter, and even year and represented in chart form to check whether key tasks constantly align with strategic goals, it will greatly reduce the presence of middlemen and improve work efficiency.

Secondly, the human resources department needs to improve the talent evaluation system to identify and eliminate middlemen and unproductive employees. In the transmission process, mid-level managers serve as information conduits. According to the information theory, each transmission of information incurs some loss. Therefore, to focus the company's overall human resources more effectively on strategic goals, overlapping institutions and information handlers should be reduced, the organizational structure should be streamlined, and the organization should be flattened to reduce the rate of information loss effectively.

In recent years, during the company's transformation process, some business splits and integrations involved adjustments to the organizational structure, which could lead to redundant work and some instances of incompetent managers. Therefore, the company's HR department will continue to sort out and optimize business functions with the aim of first reducing hierarchy and shortening the communication chain and, second, reducing redundant work to improve individual efficiency by simplifying optional tasks, thereby decreasing unproductive employees.

Finally, for new businesses, a new organizational structure should be established based on the characteristics of the new company, which will more effectively focus on core business activities, closely combining management work with business characteristics. Such integration will clarify responsibilities, authority and benefits, align talented individuals with appropriate roles, reduce the presence of middlemen and place productivity in value-creating positions. This approach ensures that everyone has a strong business orientation and that efforts are directed toward the market.

4. KEY STANDARDS FOR CONSENSUS: COMPANY VISION, MISSION AND VALUES

In a company, it is not uncommon to encounter individuals who view the company's strategy and other departmental activities with an 'outsider' or 'spectator' mindset. If they consistently maintain this mindset, it will be difficult for them to integrate into the company's strategic development. In the long run, it will be detrimental to their career. It is crucial to emphasize the importance of vision, mission and values to break this outsider mentality within the organization. Continuously using the company's vision, mission and values to select and eliminate personnel, as well as to inspire the team, helps ensure that everyone truly resonates with them and feels a sense of belonging.

In business operations, difficult decisions will inevitably arise. For instance, should a sum of money be used to purchase land or acquire a company? Which is more important and urgent? While specific problems require specific analysis, the overarching principle is to remain true to the company's original intention. The original purpose is to reach a consensus on vision, mission and values. Forgetting this intention can lead to misprioritizing tasks, resulting in busy work that ultimately does not contribute to achieving the company's vision and mission or even leads the company in the wrong direction.

In *The Innovator's Dilemma*, Harvard Business School professor Clayton Christensen describes the history of the disk drive industry. He found that well-managed industry-leading companies almost invariably failed in the next wave of innovation because they became too reliant on past successes, overly focused on meeting the needs of existing mainstream customers and neglected their original intentions and the potential for disruptive innovation.

For Digital China, a 'Digital China' is both the original aspiration and the lifelong pursuit of a lofty ideal. At its inception, the management team explored and defined this original intention through the exercise of writing epitaphs. This shared ideal united the team, enabling them to progress step-by-step from agency distribution to network, server, software services, smart city business and onto digital-cloud integration and fintech, gradually realizing their ideal. Today, Digital China remains committed to the original intention of 'Digital China,' striving to be an innovative partner and leader in the fields of digital transformation and fintech.

Twenty-five years ago, Digital China's main business was traditional distribution. However, at that time, we proposed 'Digital China,' aiming to advance China's informatization over ten, 20 and 30 years. When first formulating the company's vision, Digital China aimed to become an explorer, practitioner and promoter of 'Digital China.' As explorers, we acknowledged the possibility of sacrifices, but even if sacrifices were made, the pursuit of 'Digital China' would still hold profound significance for the Chinese nation. China missed the historic opportunities presented by the First and Second Industrial Revolutions. In the era of informatization, the Chinese nation has the full potential to leverage this industrial transformation opportunity and stand among the world's leading countries.

For over 20 years, we have continuously explored how Digital China can be a company that contributes to the nation and society and how to integrate our enterprise into the great rejuvenation of the Chinese nation. This ideal involves shouldering the responsibilities and obligations that every Chinese person of this era should undertake.

When selecting cadres at Digital China, we not only assess their capabilities but also place significant emphasis on their willingness and whether it is related to the original intention, examining whether the ambitions of the cadres align with the company's goals. Digital China believes that all employees must have a unified understanding of the original intention. Without consensus, deviations are likely to occur during the execution process.

The original aspiration of a company, as well as its vision, mission and values, are the most crucial elements in achieving consensus within the organization. The optimal state for a company is when everyone genuinely enjoys and is willing to strive for a shared vision, mission and set of values. In such a scenario, work can bring excitement and enjoyment akin to playing a game, allowing everyone to invest themselves and unleash unprecedented initiative and creativity fully.

In leading a team, we need to continuously communicate, inspire and guide everyone through both formal and informal settings. By consistently reminding ourselves and others to return to our original intentions and reach consensus, we can achieve our shared vision and mission. If we focus all our efforts on the most important tasks and align them with our core values, both individual and corporate life values will be maximized. Therefore, when you find yourself adopting an outsider mentality or when you want to help others break free from an outsider mentality, ask yourself: "What are we striving for?"

5. CONFLICTS: AN INEVITABLE PATH FOR NEWLY FORMED TEAMS

When we talk about "building the management team, setting the strategy and leading the troops," the process of leading the team often involves navigating through conflicts to reach consensus. Building trust between people takes time and requires some adjustment. Whether it is forming a new team, having an old team take on new tasks or introducing new members to a team, in a sense, it is always a process of forming a new team. Even if the people remain the same, changes in tasks and goals effectively create a new team dynamic. From the formation of a new team to becoming a cohesive and spirited group, the team must transition from the honeymoon phase to the conflict phase, then slowly integrate and finally reach the contribution phase.

Initially, there is the honeymoon phase, where everything seems perfect. During this phase, people tend to idealize each other and overlook flaws.

Soon after, the team enters the conflict phase as the initial idealization fades, and members start noticing each other's flaws, leading to conflicts. This phase is challenging and a significant test of the leadership's capability. Poor handling of this phase can lead to team disintegration.

If managed well, conflicts can lead to a series of understandings and agreements, transitioning the team into the integration phase. During this phase, adjustments in personnel might occur, forming a version 2.0 of the team.

Once integration is successful and the business is on track, the team enters the stable contribution phase. However, this phase will not be entirely free of conflict. With changing external circumstances and internal personnel dynamics, challenges in organizational management will persist.

Let's take an example from Digital China, which is launching a new proprietary brand business. This initiative will inevitably involve a process of conflict and integration. We are undertaking this new business based on a strategic decision and have some foundational business experience, making the new field less unfamiliar to us. However, the existing experience alone is insufficient. Thus, the newly formed team includes the original R&D and sales teams, some management team members from the distribution business, and externally recruited senior managers specializing in product development, supply chain and key account sales. It brings together a diverse group with significantly different working styles, thinking approaches and communication systems. The maturity of our organization is reflected in how we handle these conflicts. We must face these conflicts calmly, without getting anxious.

When faced with conflicts, it is natural for people to have emotions. However, as rational professionals, we must always keep in mind that the most important thing is to resolve the conflict, not to fear or complain about it. Since what has happened has already happened, we need to have the right mindset and take responsibility for the situation. Taking responsibility means committing to the decision and persevering until the end. The correct approach is first to determine whether the exploratory results have been achieved. If the results are in, regardless of whether they are good or bad, we share the responsibility. If the exploration is still ongoing, we must continue to find ways to improve the situation.

Exploring a new business is like a team crossing a river. If a soldier is crossing the river and you see that he is going the wrong way but do not point it out, he might correct himself, but there is a greater chance he will fall. Conversely, if you criticize him too harshly in the middle of the process and cause him to lose confidence, he is also likely to fall. Many of our tasks are similar.

As managers, we must avoid excessive criticism and provide confidence. If they lose their fighting spirit, exploration is doomed to fail. We must help them find solutions, using our broader perspective and stronger resource integration capabilities to propose more effective solutions. At the same time, we should point out their shortcomings in a factual manner rather than maintaining superficial harmony and missing the best opportunities for improvement.

As explorers of new businesses, we often face failure and criticism, which can be very frustrating. However, we must always remember that the goal is to reach the other side. Criticism during the process is not a judgement of personal worth but feedback on organizational behavior. The entire organization must take responsibility for all its innovative actions. Only in this way can the team grow and mature.

The team responsible for new business may consist of people who were originally in charge of the old business, those brought in through mergers, those transferred from different business departments, or those who were externally recruited. Forming a new team in this way is essentially a process of addressing organizational weaknesses.

Everyone is familiar with the 'barrel effect,' where the capacity of a barrel is determined by its shortest plank. If our team's cognitive abilities are lacking, the entire organizational behavior will be impaired. Therefore, we need to address these shortcomings, which inevitably lead to the formation of new teams and the emergence of conflicts.

There are no shortcuts to resolve conflicts. It requires constant confrontation to foster mutual understanding and consensus. We can use various methods and persistently communicate our message. Whether it's through kick-off meetings, special topic meetings, brainstorming sessions, democratic life meetings, celebration and recognition events, or external presentations, speeches and articles, we must utilize all available channels to convey our messages. If saying it once doesn't work, say it twice; if that doesn't work, say it three times. The fundamental task of managers is to ensure that everyone believes in what we are saying.

LEVERAGE THE DRIVING FORCE OF INCENTIVE MECHANISMS

After reaching a consensus, ensuring that this consensus continues to be effective relies heavily on the power of mechanisms. In organizational management, we must adhere to the Pareto Principle (80/20 rule). On the one hand, designing incentive mechanisms is among the 20% of tasks that are crucial in organizational management. A well-designed incentive mechanism can achieve significant results, greatly enhancing organizational efficiency. On the other hand, the design of these mechanisms aims to systematically drive employees at all levels to focus their energy on the most valuable 20% of tasks that create the most value rather than on routine matters.

I believe that, at the beginning of managing a team, every leader contemplates the issue of incentives. The market is flooded with books and courses on how to motivate teams effectively. Here, we won't delve into specific methodologies and tools, as these are akin to weapons that can be chosen based on practical needs. There's no need to overemphasize them. Instead, I want to discuss the principles of incentives. How do we establish effective incentive mechanisms? What constitutes truly effective incentives? It is crucial to understand the fundamental logic behind this.

1. SYSTEMATIC THINKING REQUIRED IN DESIGN OF INCENTIVE MECHANISMS

Just as each of us has interconnected systems – nervous, muscular, respiratory – that work together as a whole, so too must a company's various internal systems work in concert to support its external business performance. This holistic approach is the essence of systematic thinking. Similarly, employee incentives should not be considered in isolation but need to be viewed through a multifaceted, systemic lens. Systematically analysing and designing an overall incentive mechanism can benefit from models such as McKinsey's 7S Model[24] (see Figure 6-2).

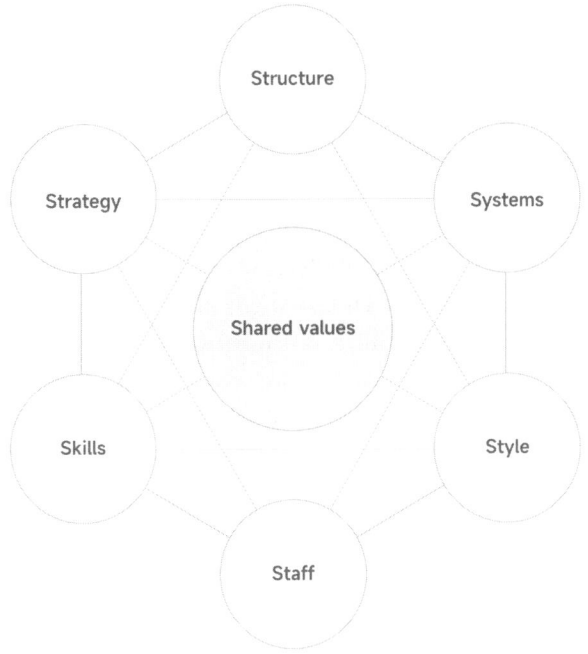

FIGURE 6-2
MCKINSEY'S 7S MODEL FOR ORGANIZATIONAL MANAGEMENT

McKinsey's 7S Model, developed in the 1980s, identifies seven internal elements of an organization that need to be aligned for success.

The 7S Model consists of seven elements, three of which are 'hard' elements: strategy, structure and systems. These elements are relatively easy to identify and can be directly influenced by management. Additionally, there are four 'soft' elements: shared values, style, staff and skills. These elements are more challenging to describe, less obvious and more influenced by company culture. However, they are just as important as the hard elements for an organization to succeed. The 7S Model is just one example. When designing incentive mechanisms, it is essential to extract the essence of excellent models like the 7S Model while ensuring they align with the specific business characteristics and current organizational situation.

A good mechanism can turn bad behavior into good behavior; a bad mechanism can turn good behavior into bad behavior. The incentive mechanisms we establish need to be visible, tangible and perceptible to everyone. That is the work of managers. During the design of these incentive mechanisms, we must develop systemic thinking skills and design from the perspective of the incentive structure. It is called an incentive mechanism rather than just simple incentives because the design must consider the entire system and multiple factors to create effective incentives. Otherwise, the incentives will fail.

When I first started working, I thought mechanism design was just for show, something to tell others about. However, as I progressed, especially through practical experience, I increasingly appreciated the importance of mechanism design. Competition is a form of management mechanism. For example, in scientific research, many research groups are divided into A and B teams, fostering competition. Why design it this way? Because no one knows the correct route, and the research outcomes of each team need to be compared. The same applies when hiring; recruiting one person to lead a new business can be uncertain, but hiring three people and comparing them can yield better results, which is a management mechanism.

Through systematic thinking, such mechanisms will form a 'system architecture.' This architecture cannot be established overnight; it requires repeated consideration and discussion, gradually developing our capabilities. For example, this chapter discusses the system architecture of leadership, which consists of four elements. These elements are not exhaustive, and their importance will change over time. If we mindlessly execute without understanding these changes, leadership will fail. However, if we can grasp the changes in these elements well, failures will be reduced.

The design of incentive mechanisms is similar. We must always maintain a systemic perspective, continuously reinforcing the concept of mechanisms. Our decisions are always made under limited conditions, determined by what we can see. As these conditions change, we must adapt our actions accordingly to progress continuously. There is no best, only better – continuous improvement and progress, which is the power of systems and mechanisms.

Digital China's incentive reforms, oriented toward value contribution, may offer some inspiration for managers.

In 2018, Digital China proposed a value-contribution-oriented incentive mechanism aiming to achieve quantitative compensation for all positions. It involved reforming the annual salary system for business operations and functional incentives, directly linking job compensation to the 'incremental contribution' of job value. On the marketing side, the department responsible for PC product sales was the first to pilot the base salary + commission incentive reform. Following this pilot, the incentive reform was widely promoted to higher levels within the department, implementing piece-rate compensation to encourage productivity and performance.

In 2019, the company further implemented its plan by introducing incremental compensation for personnel at the divisional general manager level and above. For employees, drawing on pilot experience, the incentive reform for marketing personnel was vigorously promoted in mature businesses. Different forms of base salary + commission incentive models were designed according to the various business modes and characteristics. For functional departments, workload quantification was adopted, and incentive methods were continuously promoted based on workload contributions. Additionally, long-term incentives were introduced, starting with the 2019 equity incentive plan, which granted stock options to over 200 key personnel to enhance their sense of honor and allow them to share in the benefits of the company's growth.

In 2020, the incentive reform deepened with the implementation of a company-wide value incremental compensation system. This system aimed to break down bureaucratic hierarchies, weaken the emphasis on rank, remove caps on earnings and ensure that incentive and assessment standards were fair and transparent. It allowed most employees to achieve self-management and self-motivation, directing the entire company toward a culture where more contribution led to greater rewards, thereby completely breaking away from egalitarianism. For technical personnel, the company streamlined the technical job system and capability evaluation model, promoting a dual career path (professional and managerial) for their career development. Compensation systems for technical personnel were developed according to industry standards, aligning pay with capabilities and contributions.

Since the inception of the incentive reform, the human resources department has reviewed the incentive policies of the year. Through telephone interviews, face-to-face meetings and surveys, the department tracks the effectiveness of the incentives and gathers suggestions for optimizing the policies for the following year. This systematic process of 'design – implementation – feedback – optimization' has effectively motivated business transformation and growth.

Take finance, for example. The previous reimbursement positions shifted from a fixed salary + year-end bonus incentive model to one of a base salary + commission based on the number of completed tasks. It allowed outstanding financial personnel to earn more through greater contributions, significantly improving reimbursement timeliness and service quality for employees. For the organization, this mechanism improved service quality while making the team more streamlined and efficient. In marketing, the enthusiasm of sales personnel significantly increased, and the simplified commission calculation method freed up the team's energy noticeably.

Of course, the reform of the incentive scheme is continually adjusted through ongoing trials. Different incentive methods are designed for various business models and at different stages of business development. These incentive methods guide employees toward more valuable work, promoting the principle of 'more contribution, more reward,' and are constantly being refined.

2. IDENTIFICATION OF KEY POSITIONS TO ENHANCE ORGANIZATIONAL VALUE: THE PREMISE OF INCENTIVES

In any system, there is typically a leverage point – a point where applying effort can lead to a positive feedback loop for the entire system. In the systematic design of incentive mechanisms, identifying key positions serves as this crucial leverage point. These key positions play a vital role in linking different parts of the organization, thereby helping to produce higher performance. Finding these key positions is a crucial aspect of the entire incentive process.

We aim for our company's organizational dynamics to function like a high-speed train. As everyone knows, a high-speed train is not driven by just one locomotive; each carriage has its own power system. That is how it achieves speeds of over 300 kilometres per hour. Without such a distributed power mechanism, the train could only run at 60 kilometres per hour. Key positions are akin to the power systems of each carriage in a high-speed train. Only by establishing such a power mechanism can we ensure the success of the entire company's operations.

So, who identifies what constitutes a key position? It is the first question we need to address.

Identifying key positions requires the involvement of business leaders, not the HR department. While we hope that our HR colleagues understand the business, those who have the deepest and most thorough understanding of the business are the business leaders themselves. Only those responsible for the business can determine which positions are most crucial, which talents are most scarce, and who is the most deserving of incentives.

In any business, the analysis of key positions must be based on enhancing the core capabilities of the team. Key positions will always concentrate on two areas: marketing capabilities and R&D capabilities. In R&D, the first goal is to understand the customer better and enhance the value of products and services to improve gross margins. The second goal is to improve delivery efficiency by developing new tools to reduce delivery costs. Without these two objectives, R&D lacks significance. Similarly, there is a series of tasks centred around building marketing channels and customer relationships that continually deepen the core capability of being customer-centric.

Identifying individuals for key positions aims to grasp the business better and enhance the company's value, which must be viewed within the market environment. Under market mechanisms, it is essential to identify whose output is genuinely valuable, even in uncertain conditions, rather than creating false prosperity through administrative orders.

Our business, including everyone involved, operates within the market environment, making us all market participants. As business leaders, we must continually consider how to effectively align our business with the market and enhance the company's value. Maximizing company value is the path to realizing each individual's value. In other words, by maximizing each person's value in the process, we also maximize the company's value, achieving a win-win situation for both individuals and the organization. That is the fundamental principle to grasp before designing specific incentive mechanisms.

The stakeholders of a company essentially include three groups: customers, shareholders and employees. Customers come first; without customers, the company would not exist. Next come shareholders, who provide resources and give us a platform to perform. Finally, there are employees. These three stakeholders form a triangle that requires balance. Focusing only on customer interests means the company won't be profitable or sustainable. Prioritizing only shareholder interests means employee value is not recognized. Conversely, focusing solely on employee interests without considering shareholders will result in an undervalued stock, preventing the company from scaling up. Therefore, it is crucial to find a balance among these three. As corporate managers, how do we balance these relationships? It is achieved by maximizing the organization's market value.

In the past, we viewed relationships among customers, shareholders and employees through static thinking. For example, if a business earns 10 RMB, it might allocate 3 RMB to shareholders, retain some for future customer development, and distribute 3 RMB among employees. However, now that we have entered the capital market through listing, the capital market provides a premium. This premium mechanism allows us to distribute 100 RMB from the same 10 RMB earned. These 100 RMB can be used for long-term investments, attracting more talented individuals and further increasing the company's value. Investors are willing to invest because they evaluate the business' potential and believe it has a promising future, so they are eager to share future returns with us by investing in current funds.

Therefore, when our management team considers the incentive system, the primary objective should be maximizing the enterprise's value. Only by achieving the organization's maximum value can we obtain capital premiums, thereby maximizing individual value and creating a source of motivation. Otherwise, we can only passively and statically consider profit distribution issues.

That is why we transitioned from a distribution business to a software services business. Today, we are advancing toward technology directions represented by AI and data cloud integration approaches, which are mainstream for future development. Our current efforts in fintech also include applications within the data-cloud integration technology pathways in specific industries. By integrating big data, artificial intelligence and specific scenarios, we bring new value to our customers.

Key positions and the individuals in those positions are crucial elements for enhancing our business value. If we cannot identify these key positions and people, the company's value will not improve. During strategic transformations, we face practical challenges with new businesses we don't fully understand, necessitating internal change. It involves adjustments and changes in concepts, skills, thinking patterns and behavioral norms, which can be painful. In this process, we need to bring in external talents and experts with our existing capabilities to form a combined force that maximizes organizational value.

A company must continuously evolve, stay market-oriented and open-minded, adapt to market advancements, and enhance its capabilities to keep progressing. If individuals recognize this but are unwilling to change and remain stuck in their old ways, the company faces two choices: either be dragged down by such individuals or let them go. Strategic plans need to be adjusted every three to five years based on market changes, and key positions and incentive mechanisms must be adapted accordingly. The overarching principle always focuses on enhancing organizational value.

3. EMPATHY IN MANAGEMENT: UNDERSTAND PEOPLE

Given the premises mentioned earlier, when designing specific incentive mechanisms, we must create a market-driven, effective, natural and goodwill-evoking system.

Incentive mechanisms aim to guide human behavior positively through well-designed rules. We are all familiar with Maslow's hierarchy of needs, which posits that people continuously seek to fulfil various levels of needs in their career pursuits. While individual needs may vary, common needs exist within a group. The term 'manage' in English can be broken down into 'man' and 'age,' highlighting the essence of management as addressing human maturity. When designing incentive mechanisms, it is crucial to respect human maturity and basic human nature.

The history of management theory has evolved through three stages, each based on different assumptions about human nature. The earliest wave, scientific management, emerged from the classical economic theory in England, which posited the economic man hypothesis. Under this assumption, people are rational and self-interested, with the sole purpose of working being to earn a reward. In this stage, it was believed that the only way to motivate workers was through financial incentives, with the notion that increasing monetary rewards would directly lead to higher productivity.

Over time, people found that such incentive theories were ineffective; simply having money was not enough. Karl Marx pointed out that humans are a combination of social relationships and need social interactions, respect from others, a community and spiritual comfort within a collective. That is the basis for Elton Mayo's social man hypothesis, which posits that people do not act solely for economic gain but also to maintain social status, interpersonal relationships and emotional satisfaction. Under this hypothesis, corporate management encourages employees to participate in decision-making, expand their job scopes, take on responsibilities and engage in challenging work.

Some say that Generation Y and Generation Z do not work for money and will leave a job if dissatisfied with the work environment, showing a carefree attitude. However, the same happened with Generation X when they were in their 20s. In the early years of the reform and opening-up period, many talented individuals left government positions for enterprises because they had already seen what their career paths would look like from their first day at work. Seeing their entire career trajectory from their 20s to their 60s, they found no novelty or challenge in life and were reluctant to work routinely. Once they fully committed to working in enterprises, they faced the fear of uncertainty but also embraced the challenges. It's like climbing a snowy mountain – despite the pain, they still want to climb higher. In uncertainty and the process of facing risks and challenges, people make progress and grow. The meaning of life is to challenge oneself constantly.

After several decades of development in management practice, it became clear that retaining employees through compensation and emotional connections was gradually becoming ineffective. It led to Simon's decision-making man hypothesis, which posits that each person is an autonomous decision maker. The quality of decisions depends on the decision maker's qualities and their environment. Organizations cannot make decisions on behalf of individuals but can influence personal choices by providing relevant factual and value premises. Under this hypothesis, managers believe that employee incentives should not be uniform; instead, they should be tailored to different employee types to achieve the best motivational effects.

Generally, people's needs are met progressively: as lower-level needs are satisfied, they naturally move toward higher-level needs. However, sometimes, the order of needs can shift, driven by values. For instance, the phenomenon of Lei Feng is a typical example of how he pursued higher spiritual needs despite unmet lower-level needs, which cannot be easily explained by Maslow's theory alone. His values determine this shift.

In the past, corporate organizations emphasized centralized control and ideological consistency. Today, we see that young employees have distinct personalities. Gradually, we realize that people are different, so we must learn to respect knowledge and others, which is why we emphasize the power of consensus.

Often, we tend to shift our troubles to others, assuming our perceptions represent the whole world, becoming stubborn and, coupled with arrogance and conceit, this leads to failure. If everyone could adopt an open mindset and consider whether others' knowledge could be useful, absorb and embrace diverse ideas like a sponge without quickly dismissing them, we would see a more accurate world. Personal maturity is a gradual process, as is the maturity of corporate management.

In today's diverse world, how do we motivate everyone to move forward? First, we need systematic thinking. Second, we must understand the business. Third, we must understand human nature and specific individuals. We cannot only see the trees without seeing the forest, nor can we only see the forest without seeing the trees.

Some believe that only innovative businesses can motivate employees through well-designed incentive mechanisms, but this is not true. Our company's traditional PC distribution business achieved both business growth and employee salary increases through effective incentive mechanism design. Let's analyse this case in detail below.

PC distribution was the earliest business in Digital China, and it had historically impressive revenue achievements. However, from 2015 to 2017, the scale began to decline, and over two to three years, both the overall business scale and the number of employees shrank. In such difficult circumstances, we considered improving organizational efficiency through mechanism reform to achieve business recovery and growth.

Through analysis, we found that the siloed organizational structure was the key factor restricting the development of the PC business. At that time, our PC business departments were set up based on product lines, with each product line having its own product, sales and operations departments. Departments with higher profits had more people, while those with lower profits had fewer. As the overall business scale declined, there was a significant reduction in personnel. For example, the number of people in Department H was reduced by half, leading to workforce shortages in some regions. However, due to the information-siloed organizational structure, it was impossible to redeploy personnel from other product line departments in the same area.

A typical example is the G province area of Department D. Due to low business volume, one person could fully cover the area, but this department had three people in G province. The extra two people were allocated to other provincial regions covered by Department D rather than to Departments H or L in the same G province. It is well known that sales in distribution businesses should be localized, and cross-regional work arrangements are inefficient. This product line-focused organizational structure led to overall low efficiency among sales personnel.

Apart from the uneven distribution of human resources, other issues existed. For example, different product line departments, due to competitive relationships, often withheld information or provided inaccurate information during interdepartmental communications, creating barriers and preventing departments from forming synergies.

To address these issues, we first adjusted the organizational structure. Although it was necessary to integrate and reuse personnel, we did not abruptly conduct a comprehensive integration; instead, we started with the sales department. In facing upstream manufacturers, we retained the product line-based structure to emphasize specialization, making it easier to negotiate resources with manufacturers and mitigate resistance to organizational change at the manufacturer level.

For the sales department, we integrated the business and personnel, detaching them from specific product lines. Regardless of the brand previously sold, team members were reorganized based on regions, with personnel assignments and appointment powers centralized in the sales department. Responsibilities were also unified under the sales department rather than following product lines. In the old organizational structure, channels representing multiple brands had multiple sales interfaces, resulting in resource competition and waste.

This new arrangement had several benefits. First, it allowed for the reallocation of regional sales personnel across different product lines. For example, in a province with low shipment volumes, L product line sales personnel could also support D, H and S product lines. If there was uneven personnel distribution during sales, adjustments could be made at any time. Second, it empowered channels more effectively, bringing them closer to Digital China and helping manufacturers expand channels and increase sales. Finally, individual sales personnel had more work opportunities, preventing idleness due to insufficient workload.

The organizational structure adjustment addressed the issue of rational capacity allocation. Localized, compound work for sales personnel is in line with the principle of reasonableness. However, during implementation, we encountered many challenges, such as manufacturer opposition and insufficient internal capacity building. It necessitated establishing an incentive mechanism to address team enthusiasm.

Before the incentive mechanism reform, we used an annual salary system, matching annual tasks with corresponding yearly salaries. Income was calculated based on the achievement rate of targets: 120% achievement resulted in 120% of the salary, and 80% achievement resulted in 80% of the salary. This salary system had several flaws that still haven't been completely resolved.

One issue was the reasonableness of targets, whether they were too easy or excessively demanding. Another issue was the unpredictability of external changes. Regional, product-related and other market performance factors affected sales performance. Additionally, due to low overall business gross margins, sales personnel's salary levels were generally low, and even outstanding performance differences were hard to reflect in salaries. These issues caused internal conflicts and led to the loss of excellent sales talent.

Faced with these problems, what should we do? It is well known that incentive mechanisms are central to the success of organizational structure adjustments, and all incentives start from human nature. What is human nature? Labor is human nature, and so is laziness. Most grassroots employees desire more money, less work and proximity to home. From the company's perspective, overcoming these human weaknesses requires adhering to a simple principle – more work should result in more reward. However, this work should be meritorious, genuinely adding value to the company. Therefore, we established a basic principle for incentives: within the unchanged overall incentive pool, provide more incentives to colleagues who genuinely create value for the company.

Based on this principle, we proposed the 'commission per unit sold' policy for distribution. We believed that in the PC distribution business, the gross profit per unit sold was fixed, so the commission per unit sold would reflect the value salespeople created for the company.

This policy faced significant resistance. Many thought it was too simplistic because each product had different values – how to commission for laptops versus desktops? Additionally, should regional coefficients be set? For example, should more-developed Beijing and less-developed Guizhou have different reward coefficients, given that a salesperson in Beijing might sell 100 million RMB worth of products? In comparison, one in Guizhou might sell only 10 million RMB. How do we address the unfairness caused by these influencing factors? These contradictions sparked considerable debates and conflicts.

Ultimately, after discussions, the team reached a consensus to acknowledge these irrationalities but to start implementation and gradually adjust based on the situation. Thus, the incentive method became a straightforward formula: base salary + commission per unit, ensuring that the incentive salary exceeded the fixed salary.

After implementing this incentive mechanism, interesting things happened. Previously, the sales department frequently requested more personnel from the HR department, arguing they couldn't function without more staff. A platform manager would always seek one extra person for a job that five people could handle. Now, platform managers calculate how many people are needed based on the business volume and determine their staffing. For example, for a 100 million RMB business, they might choose three people with higher salaries or five people with lower salaries. This control over staffing no longer required the intervention of headquarters but was a natural choice by the platform manager. Following this, the three-person team in G province immediately redistributed two people to other regions, significantly increasing the salary of the remaining person and serving as a strong incentive for ordinary employees.

Moreover, under a clear commission mechanism, each salesperson could clearly calculate how much income they could earn based on their efforts, directly guiding their sales behavior. Salespeople had two ways to increase their income: sell more high-traffic products or more high-commission products. For the former, they would closely monitor inventory, communicate with channels and quickly process orders upon arrival. For the latter, they would study product selling points, assess channel and product compatibility and improve channel sales capabilities. These efforts not only increased individual income but also accelerated product turnover, enhanced the sales team's product promotion awareness and abilities, and improved departmental performance. Furthermore, this reform increased customer satisfaction. Salespeople, motivated by the incentives, were willing to spend more time visiting customers, continuously learning new product knowledge, enhancing their skills and, ultimately, providing better service and improving customer experience.

Such adjustments also positively impacted the expansion of new businesses. Previously, many were reluctant to take on additional tasks because more work did not necessarily mean more pay. For example, if a salesperson's original sales target was 100 million RMB, adding a 20 million RMB task would adjust the basic target to 120 million RMB, but the income might not increase proportionally. After the reform, achieving an additional 20 million RMB in sales resulted directly in performance-based commissions, making everyone eager to secure new clients. Without adding new personnel, several new businesses we introduced quickly matched the sales of traditional product lines through development from 2018 to 2020. The salary adjustment plan is shown in Figure 6-3.

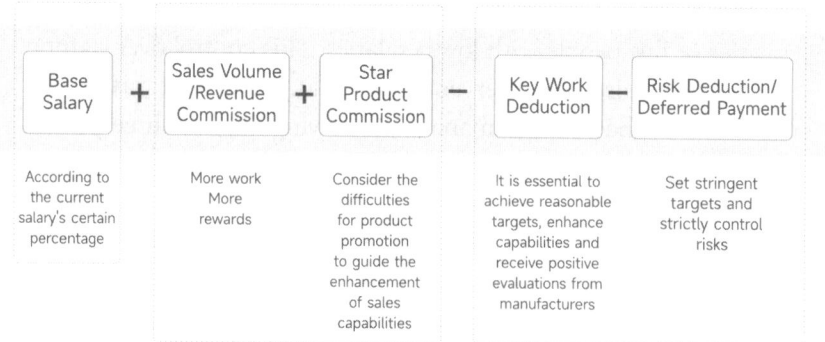

FIGURE 6-3

COMPENSATION ADJUSTMENT PLAN

While implementing positive incentives, we also established punitive measures. This design stems from the human instinct of loss aversion. People may not feel strongly about earning money, but most are very reluctant to part with it once it's in their pockets. We set up two punitive mechanisms: one is a key work deduction. If a key manufacturer needs to promote a key product, reasonable targets must be met, and failure to do so results in fines. The other is a risk deduction. If there are overdue or bad debts on orders, penalties are imposed.

Two months after adjusting the incentive mechanism, despite a 10% reduction in the total number of sales personnel and the impact of the off-season, sales revenue increased by 26% year-on-year, and the average salary per person increased by 46% year-on-year. Overall, both employees and departments benefited from this incentive reform.

In summary, there are several key reasons the organizational change and incentive system were successfully implemented.

First, the understanding and determination of the department head are crucial. Implementing change will inevitably encounter significant resistance, and there may be situations where everyone says it cannot be done. Persistence is necessary, and only with it can success be achieved.

Second, do not overlook the power of individuals during the transformation process. When their energy is unleashed, it can result in extraordinary system output. This case only described the incentives for grassroots salespeople. If we design more targeted mechanisms for mid- and senior-level managers, enabling these high-energy leaders to receive appropriate incentives, the entire organization will likely experience even greater momentum.

Third, in the process of reform, the desire for perfection is natural – we want to meet everyone's interests and satisfy various demands. However, individual interests can vary greatly. When designing mechanisms, it is essential to focus on the main objective and strive to find a win-win-win solution that benefits individuals, departments and the company. Achieving this alignment indicates a successful outcome in general.

DISCIPLINE IS COMBAT EFFECTIVENESS

If we compare the operation of a company to a car, momentum determines the direction of its movement. Transmission can be seen as the drivetrain system, where pressing the accelerator allows the engine to speed up, relying on the internal transmission of the system. The mechanism is like the engine, providing the power for the car to move forward. So, what is discipline? Discipline is the brake. When a vehicle is on the road, it stops at red lights, goes at green lights and halts for pedestrians or obstacles. Without a braking system, no one would dare to drive. Even before the appearance of cars, we spoke of unbridled horses, conveying the same principle.

Both the car and the horse analogies illustrate that any system must have constraints. Without boundaries, power becomes uncontrollable or directionless, and the system will lose control. We join an organization to showcase our talents, seek professional freedom or realize our life value. However, if we only consider individual freedom without regard for organizational discipline, doing whatever we please, the organization may cease to exist. Without foundation, what would remain? Constrained freedom is the only true freedom.

So, what is the essence of constraints for an organization?

1. THE CORE OF CONSTRAINT IS TRUST

When we were children, our parents taught us never to lie and always tell the truth. Chinese parents tell the story of the boy who cried wolf, while Western parents tell the story of Pinocchio. It demonstrates a universal human consensus on the importance of honesty. Building trust takes time, but it can be lost very quickly.

We are not only natural beings but also social beings who need to survive within social relationships and establish our credit systems. If our credit is overdrawn, even if we do good deeds in the future, people will still be sceptical. That is because others will predict future behavior based on a person's past actions. Once a negative perception of someone is formed, it is very difficult to change. Therefore, we must prevent many grey areas and use disciplinary constraints to help internal members avoid making mistakes. The ancient saying "spoiling a child is like killing a child" applies here; in an organization, if there were no disciplinary constraints and people given arbitrary authority, it would essentially provide opportunities for mistakes and be equivalent to causing harm.

On 7 July 2021, the company's human resources department issued a notice of dismissal to several employees due to their involvement in fraudulent attendance practices, such as clocking in on behalf of others or having others clock in for them. Many employees might view this issue as minor, thinking it is not a fundamental problem and questioning why it was treated as a serious violation leading to dismissal. However, we believe that integrity is crucial for both individuals and companies. If a person is willing to cheat on something as small as clocking in, what does that say about their trustworthiness? How can we trust such individuals with business responsibilities?

For organizations, the same principle of integrity holds true. We must practise self-restraint and establish a trustworthy entity, both externally and internally. Being reliable and trusted by customers is the foundation of a company's existence. As a company, the promises we make and the commitments we state must always be honored. Legal measures are primarily to protect against external issues, but our internal standard must be to fulfil our promises. This trustworthiness is the power that discipline brings.

DCITS Services has been serving Bank Q for 15 years. The partnership began with the construction of the core system. To date, five major product solutions have been implemented at the bank, achieving a customer satisfaction score of 4.98 out of 5.

Over the past ten years, the scale of contracts has grown greatly. Such a close and mutually trusted partnership relies on the service team's years of dedication, delivering trustworthy product quality, safe and stable operations, and exceeding expectations with solutions. The customer-centric service philosophy of DCITS has become ingrained in the company culture and is reflected in the daily actions of project teams.

In 2020, Bank Q faced a challenge while competing for a provincial partner project. They needed to provide an interface product with a typical development cycle of three months within just three days. Failure to deliver would result in the partner cancelling their cooperation with Bank Q.

Upholding the principle of serving the customer, DCITS took on this challenge. Bank Q expected the technical service team to develop three interfaces within two days. Faced with missing requirements, insufficient time and significant system modifications, the technical service team immediately mobilized all available architects and senior engineers to form a project group, quickly discussing and breaking down tasks. Business personnel communicated with the client to confirm interfaces and basic requirements, technical staff analysed existing systems, and testers studied the original systems. Everyone worked around the clock, and after confirming the requirements at 5 pm, they began intense design and development work.

Following the schedule to complete development and factory testing by 8 am the next day, developers and testers worked through the night. Development and integration testing was completed by 3:30 am, and after three hours of factory testing and defect corrections, the completed version was deployed to the UAT environment by 6:30 am. When contacting the bank's project team for integration testing at 8:30 am, the client was amazed: "How is it possible to deliver in such a short time?" With the successful completion of UAT testing, the three interfaces went live at 9 pm that evening.

We treat our customers' issues as our own and persistently strive to overcome challenges. This dedication has earned the trust and recognition of our clients, exemplified by the rapid growth of business with Bank Q, a benchmark client for DCITS.

At the beginning of the reform and opening-up era, Mr. Zhou Guangzhao, then president of the Chinese Academy of Sciences, once told me, "As a company, you are not only creators of material civilization but also creators of spiritual civilization. In this period of reform and opening-up, your companies should not only contribute to material progress but also set a good example in social conduct." As a company aiming for long-term success with a grand and far-reaching vision and mission, we must practise self-restraint. We cannot afford to be boastful, deceitful or hide the truth. Instead, we must steadily and honestly move forward. Even though there may be negative influences in society, we must remain true to our principles and not be swayed.

We need to establish a corporate image that embodies social responsibility, and a critical aspect is whether the organization possesses intrinsic constraints. Without internal discipline, an organization cannot be strong, and no matter how good the ideas are, they cannot be effectively implemented.

2. DISCIPLINE IS ESSENTIAL FOR EFFECTIVE CONSTRAINTS

To build a strong and combat-ready company, skilled managers often start by enforcing strict discipline to instil a sense of discipline among their subordinates. Many successful companies draw inspiration from military culture, and the core reason is to learn its strict organizational discipline. In a team, strict discipline can lead to unified thinking and consistent actions. This consistency reduces communication costs, minimizes internal friction and forms the foundation of organizational combat power. In the United States, the West Point Military Academy has produced many outstanding entrepreneurs. Why? Because organizational management requires cooperation, and to achieve efficiency in collaboration, the spirit of obedience from military culture is necessary. In uncertain or ambiguous situations, if subordinates can obey their superiors' commands, execute unconditionally, overcome difficulties and accomplish their missions, the organization will be invincible.

Without rules, there could be no order. In all aspects of life, including nation-building and governance, certain standards and laws must be followed. In a company, discipline manifests as rules and regulations. However, in actual management, many leaders spend almost no time or effort studying the discipline of organizational and work characteristics. Many managers think that as long as company regulations exist, they can enforce them on employees, sometimes even relaxing these requirements, which is effectively a voluntary relinquishment of power and strength.

For instance, performance evaluation is a typical form of discipline. Evaluation standards stem from the company's culture and values but are not immutable. These standards need to be continuously refined and discussed. Improvement is necessary not only because there is a process for digesting and absorbing standards but also because as the company grows and evolves, the understanding of the business and strategic objectives will change, leading to different talent requirements. It necessitates that managers regularly reflect on whether the current performance evaluation standards are suitable for the business and ensure that evaluations are not conducted for their own sake.

To enhance time management and ensure the timely and quality advancement of key tasks deployed by the group, Digital China's human resources department formulated the 'Digital China Weekly Report Management System,' effective from 10 February 2020. This system applies to the managers within Digital China.

The system specifies the submission method and timeline for weekly reports. Reports must be completed and submitted punctually according to the template requirements through the internal network homepage's work report system. Reports should be submitted to direct supervisors and shared with relevant personnel.

The system also outlines the quantity and quality requirements for report submissions. The human resources department conducts monthly checks on report submissions. Personnel who fail to meet the required number and quality of submissions will face serious consequences.

Since the implementation of these rules, the human resources department has consistently reported on submission rates every week. Through effective enforcement of the system, the submission rate for weekly reports has steadily increased from an initial 82% to over 99.5%.

For business managers aiming to regulate employee behavior and lead teams to achieve goals, it is essential to study and establish appropriate disciplinary measures and understand how to enforce them effectively to enhance leadership. Additionally, managers must be self-disciplined, make themselves examples, consistently adhere to and promote disciplines, and become role models for their teams. This way, employees will genuinely respect and willingly follow their leadership and directives.

During the Spring and Autumn period (770–476 BC), the concept of governing the country by virtue was highly esteemed. Confucius said, "Restrain yourself and return to the rites," which was in line with the level of social productivity at the time. Due to the simplicity of production relations and the infrequency of personnel movement, it was not necessary to rely extensively on laws; governing by virtue alone was sufficient to maintain social stability. However, as society developed and production relations became increasingly complex, by the late Spring and Autumn period, it became necessary to introduce legal constraints alongside governing by virtue. The same principle applies to organizational development. On the one hand, it is important to strengthen a shared value system; on the other hand, there must also be clear and strict disciplinary constraints to prevent the phenomenon of 'bad money driving out good.' Without discipline and without punishing or eliminating untrustworthy or problematic members, the organization is effectively punishing its contributing and capable members. If 'bad money' cannot be eliminated, the ultimate result will be a situation where everyone shares equally regardless of contribution, leading to the marginalization or voluntary departure of talented individuals.

In a business setting, good discipline creates a positive environment. Employees clearly understand the company's bottom line, which is transparent and unwavering. Managing employees is a responsibility; letting issues fester is irresponsible.

Thus, Digital China emphasizes a mechanism of survival of the fittest. Statistical results from a normal distribution show that any organization will have a few problematic individuals. It is not about judging personal worth but about organizational fit – some people will suit the organization, while others will not. For the sake of enhancing organizational efficiency, a robust and mandatory elimination mechanism is essential to remove underperforming or unsuitable individuals. It is a critical aspect of the company's disciplinary constraints. Without this, the organization will lack combat effectiveness. Digital China aims to retain qualified employees who can create value, and it will decisively deal with employees who do not pull their weight, hold them accountable, and promptly address cadres who violate regulations, neglect duties, or fail to uphold principles.

For example, to enhance the process management of marketing personnel performance, Digital China's human resources department consistently adheres to a closed-loop management approach: breaking down annual targets at the beginning of the year, signing performance agreements, conducting quarterly reviews, and identifying and eliminating underperforming personnel. At the beginning of each year, the company establishes performance agreements for each salesperson based on their performance targets and evaluation criteria and organizes the signing of these agreements. Through quarterly performance reviews, combined with the assessment of business opportunity reserves, underperforming marketing personnel are promptly identified. Employees who fail to meet performance standards for two consecutive quarters receive a performance warning letter, while those who fail for three successive quarters are subject to mandatory adjustment.

In addition to promptly eliminating unsuitable members, improving leadership and strengthening discipline, it is also crucial to enhance fundamental management. Digital China gained the understanding that 'ant holes can breach the dam' and 'details determine success or failure' after many lessons. Following the loss crisis in 2003, Digital China realized that fundamental management and risk management systems are the foundation for ensuring the company's survival. To improve fundamental management, Digital China subsequently introduced and continuously promoted the RDC plan,[25] which achieved success. However, after experiencing high growth in fiscal year 2007, fundamental management began to slacken again. There were repeated violations in both human resources and expense management, revealing that the management team was somewhat dozing off in terms of fundamental management. This slackening and negligence severely impacted the company's effectiveness and even eroded its work style and corporate culture. In this critical situation, if the gaps in discipline and management are not promptly and effectively addressed, the business, departments and even the entire company could face imminent danger. Fortunately, Digital China's subsidiaries, business units and management staff recognized the importance of strictly maintaining fundamental management and rigorous risk control. Leaders began to make themselves examples, set standards, and build a disciplined and coordinated team. Through several tough battles, they managed to pull Digital China back from the brink of danger.

Enhancing leadership also involves firmly opposing negative practices that hinder the company's development. Digital China is committed to becoming a century-old enterprise, and a crucial aspect of this goal is risk control. It includes not only managing business risks but also controlling corruption risks, which can lead to a complete collapse of the company. Corruption is akin to a cancer within an organization; it thrives when there are numerous temptations and a lack of self-awareness. Therefore, Digital China consistently reminds its internal teams to oppose corruption resolutely. Any incidents related to corruption are dealt with strictly without leniency, as this is a matter of discipline.

3. THE MOST EFFECTIVE CONSTRAINTS EMANATE FROM CORPORATE CULTURE

When discussing discipline and constraints, we often link them to corporate culture and values. Why is that? Because constraints are standards, and the formulation and implementation of these standards are determined by corporate culture. Beyond legal compliance, corporate culture dictates the behavioral norms within an organization. So, what is corporate culture?

Once, someone asked Qian Zhongshu[26] what culture is. He was momentarily stumped and pondered for a long time before offering an answer: "Culture is our collective memory." For instance, *Records of the Grand Historian* (*Shiji*) is a historical account that records everything from myths and legends to the Zhou, Qin and Han dynasties. It represents the shared memory of the Chinese nation, profoundly impacting our entire ethnic group. Without *Shiji*, no one could remember so much, and culture would be difficult to pass down.

Similarly, in a company, corporate culture is akin to our shared memory of development. Everything we have today, whether good or bad habits, is a product of our developmental history. Past successes influence current behavioral patterns and form the foundational color of the company's heritage. For example, the contracting system has contributed to stable profits for our company over a long period, which is a very successful experience. However, it may not be suitable for future innovative businesses, and we must make painful adjustments. During the enforcement of new disciplines, if lax enforcement is enforced, it can lead to a lack of seriousness about the discipline.

Why does lax enforcement occur? It is often due to dilemmas in the enforcement process.

There was a fascinating story that took place during Shang Yang's reforms.[27] At that time, the ruler of the Qin State was Duke Xiao of Qin, who appointed Shang Yang to carry out the reforms and provided extraordinary support. However, Duke Xiao's son committed a crime, and according to the law, he was supposed to be punished. This situation put Shang Yang in a difficult position because he was the only son of Duke Xiao. If Shang Yang were to depose him, the Qin State would have no heir. Without an heir, the purpose of the reforms – to ensure the long-term prosperity of the Qin State – would be undermined. After all, what would be the point of prosperity and strength if there were no successor? On the other hand, if Shang Yang did not enforce the punishment, the law would lose its deterrent effect and essentially become meaningless.

In this challenging situation, Shang Yang found a compromise. He punished the Grand Mentor of the Crown Prince, Ying Qian, who was also Duke Xiao's elder brother and a staunch supporter of the reforms. Shang Yang cut his nose off as a punishment. Although the Grand Mentor was obviously unhappy, he still supported Shang Yang's decision and did not refuse to enforce the law due to his status. After this incident, the implementation of the rule of law in Qin proceeded without further obstruction, laying a solid foundation for the strengthening of the Qin State.

Therefore, adhering to principles is often a significant test for leaders, as it gauges their commitment to upholding standards. When dealing with issues, decisions should be made swiftly, but when addressing personnel matters, caution is essential, as many problems are not as straightforward as they appear. In the process of company development, handling such dilemmas creates a deep collective memory.

The impact of these memories on everyone can be even greater than the influence of the discipline itself. Ultimately, what people remember is the incident, not necessarily the enforcement process. However, regardless of how we handle these situations, we must remember that all disciplinary actions target the issue itself to ensure that everyone understands not to cross the line rather than target individuals.

So, what should we do? First, we must ensure strict enforcement of the rules. Second, effective communication about these matters is crucial; everyone needs to clearly understand that we are resolute in following the rules. While this sounds straightforward, balancing this in practice is challenging and requires wisdom. Whether it's discipline or mechanisms, it may require breaking away from past successful experiences, denying or transforming them, and overcoming organizational inertia, which is very difficult and demands strong conviction.

In addition to having conviction, our rules must be reasonable and practical. If the rules do not align with the actual situation, they are difficult to enforce and leave room for discretion. Therefore, developing rules that are both reasonable and aligned with our business needs is a challenging task.

Under the contracting system, rule formulation was relatively simple; for example, allocating a profit target of 100 million RMB among ten managers, with each manager responsible for 10 million RMB. However, for refined management involving process mechanism development, we need to decompose the profit target process. It consists in breaking down the various tasks required to achieve the result across different positions, assigning these responsibilities accordingly, and establishing incentives or penalties based on these roles. Otherwise, we risk continuing with a coarse management approach where processes remain uncontrollable. This decomposition tests the leader's expertise; if done improperly, no one will truly be accountable for the results, making decomposition ineffective. Conversely, focusing solely on results without process decomposition will hinder the organization's effectiveness. Thus, we now encourage specialization and structural breakdown, which is a challenging but correct path.

Exploring mechanisms requires a process of advocating, standardizing and enforcing discipline. For instance, we have implemented weekly time management reports for over five years, but there is still room for improvement. At the beginning of implementation, it would not be appropriate to impose penalties for failing to submit reports. Individual coaching is a better approach, providing necessary pressure while allowing gradual improvement. Once reports reach a certain level of consistency, they can be enforced as a discipline.

Throughout the entire process of developing and implementing mechanisms, all members of the organization must practise self-discipline. Facing challenges and difficulties requires addressing and self-regulation, which can be painful for everyone, including myself. At such times, maintaining the right attitude is crucial. As a leadership team, especially our executive members, we must lead by example and practise self-discipline. We should first adhere to the standards set for our employees so that we can approach our responsibilities with a more positive and proactive mindset.

CHAPTER 7
EFFECTIVENESS AND BALANCE ARE THE ULTIMATE MEANING OF TIME MANAGEMENT

FOCUS ON HIGH EFFICIENCY BUT EMPHASIZE HIGH EFFECTIVENESS

Over the years, I have been advocating for time management, implementing time management concepts in the company under great pressure, and organizing time management training. It is not just to get more things done in a limited amount of time; I want to emphasize that everyone should not only pursue efficiency but also recognize the importance of effectiveness for both individuals and the enterprise.

In management, efficiency refers to the amount of work completed per unit of time or the ratio of the results obtained from a particular task to the time and workforce spent on it. It is about using social resources effectively to meet human desires and needs. Effectiveness refers to the efficiency and results displayed in purposeful and organized activities. It reflects the correctness of the activity goals chosen and the degree to which they are achieved. It is the balance between output and capacity, as well as the balance between short-term interests and long-term goals.

In real life, we often see that both enterprises and individuals mainly focus on efficiency.

For example, managers always want employees to put in extra effort to accomplish a task as quickly as possible. However, if we take a step back and think carefully, we might find that the task is not that important to the company. It might even overly consume the company's resources, preventing them from being allocated to genuinely needed business areas. Although this approach may appear to achieve high efficiency, it actually does not bring any effectiveness to the company.

For another example, some people love reading, but they do so superficially without thinking deeply. They pursue the quantity of books they read, believing that the more and the faster they read, the better. But does this bring them true growth? No, because they do not absorb the essence of the books. The knowledge in the books does not sink in, let alone become internalized as their thoughts.

Peter Drucker succinctly summarized efficiency and effectiveness in his book *The Effective Executive* as, "Efficiency is doing things right; effectiveness is doing the right things." According to him, efficiency and effectiveness should not be neglected, but this does not mean they are equally important. Ideally, we aim to improve both efficiency and effectiveness, but when they cannot both be achieved, we should focus on effectiveness first and then work on improving efficiency.

Herbert A. Simon, a management scientist and Nobel laureate, also provided a comprehensive analysis of the distinction between efficiency and effectiveness. He believed that efficiency improvement primarily relies on work methods, management techniques and some reasonable norms, plus leadership skills. However, to improve effectiveness, one must have policy insight, strategic vision, exceptional judgement and planning abilities.

It is evident that while efficiency is important, we should not mindlessly pursue it. High effectiveness is truly worth pursuing. For example, in a company, there might be two employees doing the same job. One is busy all day, filling a page with tasks, seemingly very efficient but not creating much value for the company. The other appears less busy but focuses well on key tasks and solves many problems for the company, creating significant value. Which employee would the manager value more? The answer is, of course, the latter because he is both efficient and effective.

High effectiveness is the true goal of our time management. Effective time management allows us to plan our goals and outcomes, preventing us from falling into the trap of merely pursuing efficiency. For instance, many internet companies do not prioritize profitability in their early stages, often operating at a loss for a long time. However, they focus on accumulating traffic and increasing market shares. They temporarily forgo immediate benefits for future sustained growth, pursuing high effectiveness rather than short-term efficiency.

Efficiency represents speed and quantity, while effectiveness represents quality and sustainability. Time management helps us persist in dedicating time to truly valuable activities that bring high effectiveness. This approach will have a positive and far-reaching impact on our lives and our enterprises. *The McKinsey Way* states that doing things right emphasizes efficiency, resulting in moving us faster toward our goals. Doing the right things emphasizes effectiveness, ensuring that our work steadily progresses toward our goals. Efficiency focuses on the best way to complete a task, while effectiveness focuses on the optimal use of time.

BALANCE WORK AND LIFE

Balancing work and life is also a crucial objective of time management. If we view an enterprise as an energy entity, what state would be the most ideal? If I were to answer in one word, I believe that word would be "balanced."

Many people pour a tremendous amount of time and energy into their careers, operating at full capacity amid a mountain of work. Yet, they neglect their lives, ignoring the cultivation of family and personal relationships.

Work and life are not mutually exclusive; work is inherently a part of life. To maintain long-term enthusiasm for work, one must learn to organize one's life reasonably. If you are constantly on edge because of work every day, you will only deplete yourself, falling into a state of anxiety and fatigue. How can such a person find a sense of accomplishment in their work?

In sociology, there is a theory called the Total Happiness Theory, which suggests that the happiness people feel is accumulated across different dimensions and is not measured by a single indicator. Work and life occupy different dimensions in our lives, both of which are indispensable. Only by improving the quality of both can we achieve greater happiness. A healthy lifestyle leads to high work efficiency, and efficient work provides ample energy to enhance the quality of life. In a sense, a healthy lifestyle is a prerequisite for good work. When the larger context is stable, you will have the drive to work and feel the value of life.

Therefore, we should not draw a dividing line between work and life. We must learn to coordinate between the two, seeking balance and mastering the rhythm of fast and slow, living a life with both relaxation and tension.

So, how can we master the art of balancing work and life?

1. ALLOCATE TIME FOR FAMILY

If you're meeting an important client and your wife calls, saying, "It's time to pick up the kids," you'll likely feel torn, and your wife will be equally frazzled. Therefore, when planning your time, it is crucial to consult with family members and gain their understanding and support, especially those of your spouse. Both partners must have an awareness and practice of balancing family and career, sharing family responsibilities, coordinating schedules, and reasonably allocating time and energy. When one partner is busy, the other can take on more family duties during their less busy times. Only through mutual efforts can you achieve a balance between family and career.

To help employees create a warm family atmosphere, Digital China has established a dedicated Outdoor Family Day and organized a variety of Health Week activities. Outdoor Family Day involves activities such as hiking, camping and mountain climbing, where employees and their families can participate, promoting interaction and sharing among employees from different business units. The Health Week activities include both team competitions and individual fun events, allowing everyone to enjoy the fun of sports and spread enthusiasm for physical activity. These activities have received widespread acclaim from employees.

---

2. ALLOCATE TIME FOR REST

Farmers understand the nature of the land: Despite its rich resources, it needs a period of nurturing to yield the best results. Workers know that a bowstring cannot remain taut without a break. Likewise, humans must follow the laws of nature; only by resting well can we maintain good health, a cheerful mood and abundant energy.

Many people achieve remarkable results in their work, not by sacrificing rest but rather by valuing it. They win health and vitality by prioritizing rest, which forms the foundation of their success.

Mr. Feng Youlan, a renowned philosopher of the 20th century, was born on 4 December 1895 and passed away at the age of 95 on 26 November 1990. His secret to longevity was timely rest. Although he worked tirelessly, he never overextended himself. After a period of desk work, he would take a break, tend to his plants or go for a walk to adjust his state of mind.

Achieving high-quality rest is not an easy task. The biggest obstacle is that people often find it difficult to focus entirely on work when it's time to work and to decisively set aside their work to rest when it's time to rest. No matter how busy we are, it is rarely the case that we have absolutely no time for rest. What is more concerning than a tight schedule is the stress from work that we carry into our personal lives, burdening us every second. During rest, our minds often cannot relax as we continue to think about work-related issues. Even when we are away from computers and files, our lives remain closely tied to these tasks, preventing complete rest. This tension can even invade our sleep, preventing relaxation. Over time, this lack of rest can lead to health problems. Instead, it is better to adjust our mindset in a timely manner: diligently work when it's time to work and completely relax when it's time to rest.

3. ALLOCATE TIME FOR HEALTH

Health is the source of life. Without it, all the wealth in the world would be merely symbolic, and all pursuits could be just slogans. Many people ignore their physical well-being, leading to the tragic situation of 'dying before their aspirations are fulfilled.' They may appear prematurely old despite being in the prime of their lives. Their lives become dull and uninspiring, destroying their potential for achievement, which is a profound sadness.

The body is a lifelong companion, and treating it well is treating life well. Having a healthy body and a sound mind is the greatest happiness in life. Therefore, we must allocate time for health. Health is not just the absence of diseases or pain; it involves maintaining a state of complete physical, mental and social wellbeing. It means that a healthy person should have a strong physique, an optimistic mental state, and the ability to maintain harmonious relationships with society and the natural environment.

Digital China organizes a variety of cultural and sports activities each year, including 'Badminton Day' and the 'Digital China Cup' soccer and basketball tournaments. Additionally, Digital China has established swimming and badminton clubs to support employees in pursuing hobbies and staying fit. These events and activities not only foster a strong awareness of fitness among employees and serve as an effective outlet for stress relief, but also create a platform for communication and interaction across business units and departments, receiving enthusiastic feedback from employees.

Additionally, to prevent illnesses from affecting employees' quality of life, the Digital China Union has established a Mutual Aid Fund. Initiated by the Digital China Labor Union and open to voluntary employee participation, the Mutual Aid Fund provides crucial support when faced with illness-related risks. It brings a touch of warmth and reduces hardship, offering more protection and lessening uncertainties.

4. ALLOCATE TIME FOR REFLECTION

However busy we are, we must allocate time for reflection, especially when faced with important issues or significant strategic decisions. When confronted with a particularly challenging strategic decision, I usually prefer to avoid making an immediate decision and instead give it some time to think over: "Is this really the case?" Similarly, if something seems particularly advantageous, it's wise to pause and consider: "Is this really true? Why would I be so lucky? Could this be a trap?" Nothing is absolute; everything has two sides, and we need to ponder from multiple angles.

Rhythm is a form of harmony found everywhere in nature and social life. Nature has its tides, sunrises and sunsets, and seasonal changes. Plants sprout, grow, mature and spread seeds. Human society continuously evolves from primitive stages to higher ones. Work and life also have their own rhythms. Only through time management can one master the rhythm of work and life, allowing for a balanced and effortless approach. This mastery enables one to create a harmonious symphony of work and life, achieving inner value in work while also experiencing happiness and satisfaction in life.

PLAN BEFORE TAKING ACTION TO MITIGATE RISKS

Another benefit of time management is the ability to plan ahead, thereby reducing the probability of unexpected events and risks.

'Plan before you act, and you will always succeed.' This principle from ancient Chinese military strategy is highly valued. Modern enterprise management should adopt the same approach. The internal and external environments of an enterprise are constantly changing, presenting various issues and challenges. Managers need to plan strategically to reduce the likelihood of unexpected events and risks, solving problems through careful planning.

In 2020, Digital China undertook the delivery of a big data platform for a specific industry in City A. This project, as a benchmark for municipal big data platforms, was crucial for securing two additional big data projects in the same region and expanding opportunities for three other city-level big data projects. Its success was significant both for the client and the company's business expansion. The smooth delivery of this project was a result of thorough planning facilitated by effective time management.

The project requirements emerged in March 2020, with a clear deadline for acceptance and delivery by July, making it a tight schedule with heavy tasks. That is where Digital China's efficient time management came into play: on 14 March, we dispatched a three-person research team to the project site to start the requirements analysis. By 16 April, we had completed the internal requirements design review report for the client, and on 6 May, provincial and municipal experts gave high praise during the design scheme review. On 11 June, we presented and demonstrated the latest research results to the responsible leaders, gaining high recognition from them.

Throughout the project, the team adhered to the goal of completing the final acceptance within 90 calendar days by breaking it down into weekly and monthly plans, 'focusing on the lighthouse and steering accordingly,' and constantly adjusting the course. Issues involving coordination with multiple parties were meticulously planned, communicated and deployed in advance. By combining parallel construction with accelerated work, the project was ensured to meet milestone nodes on schedule. This journey from zero to completion was one of continuous exploration and expansion. The management team's foresight allowed the project to overcome numerous unexpected challenges and achieve smooth delivery.

In terms of results, the project took a total of three months from requirements analysis to initial deployment. The 13-person project team created a nationally leading, locally distinctive municipal-level industry big data demonstration project, receiving high praise from the client and providing critical support for securing the next phase of the project. Additionally, the project standardized and formulated products for city-level big data platforms in the industry, providing strong support for the company's market expansion in other regions.

When managers make decisions, they should approach them with the same careful consideration as military strategy and tactics: think thoroughly before acting. Through preparatory work, they should study the facts, gather materials and information, understand the ins and outs of the tasks, and then formulate appropriate plans and strategies based on this research. In summary, by understanding the development scenarios and characteristics of situations and grasping their direction, one can effectively reduce the likelihood of unexpected events and risks by planning before taking action.

In many cases, much of the work can be arranged in advance. For example, major undertakings such as investments and mergers and acquisitions may take a year or even a year and a half to complete, with very complex tasks involved. It requires early planning – the sooner, the better, as the probability of unexpected events and risks decreases. Every major acquisition by Digital China is essentially a major innovation because each one involves doing things that have not been done before. Through this process, Digital China has gained a key insight: by planning ahead, thoroughly considering risk factors, and managing the overall pace and timeline of tasks, it can avoid or significantly reduce the pressure of completing urgent work within very short time frames. This approach enables smoother and more manageable workflows. By controlling the overall rhythm and time allocation of work, we can avoid or reduce the need to complete urgent tasks in a short period, thereby making the overall workload more manageable.

From the perspective of modern risk-control theory and practice, focusing on the latent phase of risks is crucial for effectively reducing the probability and impact of risks. During this phase, risks are still submerged and can be detected and controlled. Therefore, risk management at this stage should focus on prevention, with the primary task being thorough planning and preparation. It involves identifying potential risks, avoiding and transferring risks, and reducing the probability of occurrence. Additionally, it is essential to prepare for contingency plans. When risks inevitably arise, these preparations provide a foundation for emergency handling, allowing us to respond, manage and mitigate the aftermath with relative ease.

China's commercial integrity system is still in the process of continuous improvement. Risks are ubiquitous – whether in the past, present or future. The risk-management system has always been a core component of Digital China's competitive edge. Years of practice have proven that it is the guarantee that keeps Digital China invincible and the key to the healthy development of the organization. Therefore, Digital China does not collaborate with individuals or organizations that do not adhere to commercial principles and always maintains a vigilant awareness of risk prevention at all times.

Of course, risk management is not about stifling business operations. The key is to leverage advantages and achieve mutual growth for the enterprise and its clients. As business managers, we must implement effective risk management measures to maximize the potential of the company's limited resources. It involves acquiring strong, creditworthy and valuable clients while maintaining good financial health and minimizing operational risks.

Risk management capabilities rely on organizational support, institutional processes and individual abilities. In this regard, establishing risk-management organizations at various levels is a hallmark of Digital China. Only through continuous process and system development, attention to detail and the implementation of effective responsibilities can potential issues be nipped in the bud. Furthermore, strengthening our service capabilities – being familiar with the business and extending to the business frontlines – enables us to proactively, accurately and effectively support the continuous evolution and optimization of business operations, thereby enhancing overall core competitiveness. For example, we should place great emphasis on client visits. During conversations with clients, they often provide valuable information that can then be used to plan future actions.

In the rapidly changing, highly competitive and fast-developing technology industry, opportunities can disappear in an instant. Technology companies must be proactive – seeing, thinking and acting earlier than others. They should be able to manage current tasks while preparing for future opportunities, like simultaneously eating from a bowl, cooking in a pot and planting in a field. For technology companies, maintaining a high-level perspective and planning well in advance is the best strategy. Only by staying vigilant, seizing opportunities and relying on strategic thinking can an overall competitive advantage be achieved.

REFERENCES

1. Brynjolfsson, Erik, and Andrew McAfee. *The Second Machine Age*. Translated by Jiang Yongjun. Beijing: CITIC Press Group, 2014.
2. Drucker, Peter. *The Practice of Management*. Collectible Edition. Translated by Qi Ruolan. Beijing: Machinery Industry Press, 2009.
3. Drucker, Peter. *The Effective Executive*. Translated by Xu Shixiang. Beijing: Machinery Industry Press, 2005.
4. Franklin, Benjamin. *The Autobiography of Benjamin Franklin*. Translated by Pu Long. Nanjing: Yilin Press, 2009.
5. Granin, Daniil. *A Peculiar Life*. Translated by Hou Huanhong and Tang Qici. Zhengzhou: Haiyan Press, 2001.
6. Guo Wei. *The Power of Digitization*. Beijing: Machinery Industry Press, 2022.
7. Simon, Herbert A. *Administrative Behavior*. Translated by Zhan Zhengmao. Beijing: Machinery Industry Press, 2013.
8. Marx, Karl, and Friedrich Engels. *The Collected Works of Marx and Engels*, Vol. 1. Translated by the Compilation and Translation Bureau of the Central Committee of the Communist Party of China. Beijing: People's Publishing House, 2009.
9. Christensen, Clayton. *The Innovator's Dilemma*. Translated by Hu Jianqiao. Beijing: Citic Press, 2020.
10. Parkinson, Northcote. *Parkinson's Law*. Translated by Chen Xiuzheng. Beijing: SDX Joint Publishing Company, 1982.
11. Mayo, George Elton. *The Social Problems of an Industrial Civilization*. Translated by Shi Kan. Beijing: Machinery Industry Press, 2016.
12. Robbins, Stephen. *Organizational Behavior*. 18th ed. Translated by Sun Jianmin, Zhu Xiji, and Li RMB. Beijing: China Renmin University Press, 2021.

13. Sun Tzu. *The Art of War*. Annotated by Chen Xi. Beijing: Zhonghua Book Company, 2022.

14. Tagore, Rabindranath. *The Religion of Man*. Translated by Zeng Yuhui. Changsha: Hunan People's Publishing House, 2017.

15. Peters, Tom, and Robert Waterman. *In Search of Excellence*. Translated by Hu Weishan. Beijing: Citic Press, 2015.

16. Sowell, Thomas. *Basic Economics*. Translated by Wu Jianxin. Chengdu: Sichuan People's Publishing House, 2018.

17. Wu Jing. *Essentials of Governance of the Zhenguan Reign*. Beijing: China Literature and History Press, 1999.

18. Xi Jinping. *The Governance of China*, Vol. 1. Beijing: Foreign Languages Press, 2018.

19. Project Management Institute. *A Guide to the Project Management Body of Knowledge (PMBOK Guide)*. 6th ed. Beijing: Publishing House of Electronics Industry, 2018.

20. Smith, Adam. *The Wealth of Nations*. Collectible Edition. Translated by Tang Risong. Beijing: Huaxia Publishing House, 2012.

21. Yan Weimin, and Wu Weimin. *Data Structures: C Language Edition*. Beijing: Tsinghua University Press, 2007.

22. Yang Kuan. *A Chronological Compilation and Annotation of Historical Materials of the Warring States Period*. Shanghai: Shanghai People's Publishing House, 2001.

23. Wei Linwei. "The Latest Advances in Project Management." *Journal of Management Engineering*, 2000, no. 3.

ENDNOTES

1. Digital China Group Co., Ltd. (Stock Code: 000034. SZ), hereafter referred to as Digital China.
2. Sowell, T. (2018). *The Economic Way of Thinking* (W. Jianxin, Trans.). Sichuan People's Publishing House.
3. In modern management, directed graphs are often used to describe and analyse the planning and implementation process of a project. A project is typically divided into several smaller subprojects, known as activities. In a weighted directed graph, vertices represent events, directed edges represent activities, and the weights on the edges represent the duration of the activities. This type of graph is abbreviated as an AOE Network. It helps us better understand the significance of time management in team collaboration.
4. Digital China Holdings: A Hong Kong-listed company specializing in IT services and digital solutions. Its stock is traded under the ticker 00861.HK. Digital China Holdings provides a wide range of digital transformation services and technology solutions across various industries, aiming to drive digital innovation in China.
5. The date, 11 November (11/11), was chosen because the numeral one resembles a bare stick, known in Chinese as *guanggun*, which is figuratively compared to an unmarried man, who doesn't add 'branches' to the family tree, making the tree trunk appear like a bare stick.
6. There is some disagreement in the field of management studies regarding the division of management functions. Henri Fayol, the founder of classical organizational theory in France, mentioned five elements of management in his book, *General and Industrial Management (Administration Industrielle et Générale)*: planning, organizing, commanding, coordinating and controlling. However, Stephen Robbins, an American management expert, asserts in his book, *Management*, that management includes four elements: planning, organizing, leading and controlling. The author believes that the concepts of leadership

7. Digital China Information Service Group Co., Ltd., referred to as DCITS, is public-listed in Shenzhen, China (Stock Code: 000555.SZ), providing fintech services as driven by Data Cloud Integration Strategy.

8. A Gantt chart is a project management visualization tool, which will be elaborated on in Chapter 5.

and management are parallel with some overlap, rather than a relationship of inclusion, and that the content of commanding can be encompassed within planning and coordinating, making it unnecessary to propose it separately. Therefore, the author proposes four major functions of management.

9. The concept of bounded rationality was introduced by Herbert Simon, also known as scientific decision-making. Simon was the first to propose combining artificial intelligence with decision science and is a Nobel Laureate in Economics. His vast knowledge and broad research interests made him one of the founders of many significant academic fields. Throughout his life, he earned nine doctoral degrees, marking him as an extraordinary scientist. Additionally, he was one of the founders of the Graduate School of Industrial Administration at Carnegie Mellon University.

10. In Digital China, 'branch' refers to regional branch operations such as 'Shanghai Branch' or 'Chengdu Branch.'

11. Business Intelligence (BI) refers to the use of modern data warehouse technology, online analytical processing (OLAP), data mining and data visualization techniques to analyse data and achieve business value. The concept of BI became widely understood through Howard Dresner's popularization in 1989. At that time, BI was defined as a category of technologies and applications aimed at aiding business decision-making, comprising components such as data warehouses (or information marts), query and reporting, data analysis, data mining, data backup and recovery.

12. Legge, J. (Trans.). (n.d.). "Great Learning" from *The Book of Rites*. Retrieved from https://ctext.org/liji/da-xue.

13. 'Channel' in Digital China Group refers to downstream distributors in the distribution business, with 'core channels' indicating key distributors with large sales volumes.

14. Zeno's paradox, documented in Aristotle's book *Physics*, became known to later generations.

15. "Ensure benefits flow through one channel" originates from *Guanzi* and describes how centralized benefits strengthen a nation. Inspired by this principle, the founder and CEO of Huawei Technologies Ren Zhengfei added, "Concentrate efforts in one direction" to emphasize both focused effort and benefit in a corporate context.

16. Data cloud integration, introduced by Digital China in 2022, is based on its deep expertise in the IT industry developed over the past 20 years. This concept not only reflects Digital China's strategic vision and insights into enterprise digital transformation but also represents its own digital strategy and planning.

17. The data comes from the annual "China Banking IT Solutions Market Share" report published by the authoritative consulting firm IDC.

18. Transaction consistency refers to the need for a database system to maintain logical consistency when performing a series of operations to complete a real business transaction. For example, in the banking transaction logic of "transferring 100 RMB from John Doe's account to Jane Doe's account," the database system needs to perform the operations of "deducting money from John Doe's account" and "adding money to Jane Doe's account." If the first operation is completed but the second operation is not, the bank's database would lose 100 RMB out of thin air, rendering the system untrustworthy. Therefore, ensuring transaction consistency is a crucial security standard for the core banking system.

19. The *Zuo Zhuan* (*Zuo Commentary*), specifically in the "Tenth Year of Duke Zhuang" chapter, is a part of one of the earliest Chinese historical texts that provide detailed commentary on the Spring and Autumn annals. The events recorded in this chapter revolve around various political and military manoeuvres among the states during the Spring and Autumn period.

20. The Grand Canal of China, a UNESCO World Heritage site, is the longest and oldest canal in the world, stretching from Beijing to Hangzhou. It was initially constructed in sections as early as the 5th century BC, but it was Emperor Yang of the Sui dynasty in the 7th century AD who initiated its major expansion, transforming it into a vast network that played a crucial role in China's history as a major transportation route for goods, people and culture.

21. PMBOK stands for Project Management Body of Knowledge, a set of standards and best practices for project management by the Project Management Institute (PMI). It outlines key process groups and knowledge areas, and serves as a primary reference for PMI certifications like the Project Management Professional (PMP).

22. Unified Modeling Language (UML) is a nonproprietary third-generation modeling and specification language. UML is an open method used to specify, visualize, construct and document the artifacts of a software-intensive system under development, particularly for object-oriented systems. UML represents a collection of best engineering practices that have proven successful in modeling large-scale, complex systems, especially at the software architecture level.

23. Michael Yu, also known as Yu Minhong, is a Chinese entrepreneur and educator, best known as the founder of New Oriental Education & Technology Group, one of China's largest private educational service providers. Born in 1962, Yu started his career as an English teacher before establishing New Oriental in 1993. He is widely recognized for his contributions to education and his inspirational journey from humble beginnings to becoming a leading figure in China's private education sector.

24. McKinsey's 7S Model was developed by consultants at McKinsey & Company, notably by Tom Peters and Robert Waterman, in the early 1980s.

25. From 2004 to 2006, the company focused its efforts on the RDC project, which can be translated into English as Rebuild Digital China. The three letters in RDC have deeper meanings: R stands for risk management; D represents development, referring to human resources management; and C signifies customer, indicating a shift toward a customer-centered service transformation. We believe that these three aspects are crucial capabilities for the company.

26. Qian Zhongshu: A prominent Chinese scholar, writer and literary critic, best known for his novel *Fortress Besieged* (*Wei Cheng*). Born in 1910, Qian was renowned for his deep knowledge of both Chinese and Western literature, and his works continue to influence Chinese literary and academic circles.

27. Shang Yang's Reforms: Implemented during the Warring States Period (475–221 BC) in the State of Qin, these reforms, led by the statesman Shang Yang in the 4th century BC, were aimed at strengthening the state's military and economic power. They included measures such as land redistribution, centralization of power, legal standardization, and a merit-based system for military and civil service. Shang Yang's reforms significantly contributed to the rise of Qin, eventually leading to its unification of China.

ABOUT THE AUTHOR

GUO WEI

Chairman, Digital China Group Co., Ltd., Chairman, Digital China Information Service Group Company Ltd., Chairman of the Board of Directors, Digital China Holdings Limited, and author of *The Power of Digitalization* (Chinese version), *The Power of Datafication* (English version) and *The Power of Time*.

    Mr. Guo Wei is the founder of Digital China. Under his vision and leadership, Digital China has taken the lead in idea, technology, and practice since its establishment in 2000, and has become the leading digital transformation partner in China. He has empowered the digital transformation of the industry with independently innovated core technologies. Furthermore, Digital China is an indisputable market leader in the vertical industry sectors including digital industry, fintech, and has consistently outpaced its competition, committed to becoming a leading partner of digitalization in China. In 2024, Digital China was ranked among the Fortune China 500 list for the eighth consecutive year, included in the Fortune China All-Star List of Most Admired Companies for the second consecutive year, and recognized by Forbes China as one of the Top 50 Influential Fintech Companies and a Leading Enterprise in Digital Technology.

Mr. Guo Wei cultivated the aspiration of building a 'digital China' and put it into practice through his over three-decade endeavor in the IT and digital technology industry. His visionary theoretical research and extensive industry practice are widely acknowledged. He was awarded the Qiu Shi Achievement Award for Outstanding Young People by China Association for Science and Technology, the WEF's Leaders of Future Economy in China, the Ten Outstanding Young Persons in China, the Great Names in Software since Chinese Economic Reform, the Software Figures of the Decade, Top Ten Leaders in China's Software and Information Service Industry, Top Ten People of the Year for Fintech in China 2023, the Ram Charan Management Practice Award 2023, etc. In addition, he has been selected as one of China's 50 Most Influential Business Leaders released by *Fortune China* for three consecutive years.

Moreover, he served as a member of the 11th & 12th CPPCC National Committee and the 4th Advisory Committee for State Informatization (ACSI); vice president of the Digital China Industry Alliance; vice chairman of the Society of Management Science of China; member of the Advisory Committee for Industrial Transformation, Institute of Internet Industry, Tsinghua University; Adjunct professor of Northeastern University and managing director of the Board of Trustees, Ph.D. Supervisor of Hong Kong Financial Services Institute, etc.

Mr. Guo Wei has published several books, including *The Power of Digitalization*, *The Power of Time*, *The Power of Datafication*, co-authored *The Power of Finance*, *Chinese Smart City Construction Guidelines and Best Practices*, and also has been invited to compile a series of professional books on financial technology published by People's Publishing House, such as *15 Lectures on FinTech*, *Digital Economy Technology for Good – Financial Technology Innovation Practice 2021*, *Financial Innovation Helps Achieve Common Wealth* and *Integrating Digital and Real Economy: Fintech Innovation Practice*.

BY THE SAME AUTHOR

ISBN: 978-1-915951-51-9